# Confessions

Scottish Criminal Law and Practice Series

*Series Editor*

The Rt Hon The Lord McCluskey

# Confessions

David B Griffiths LLB, PhD, NP
Solicitor

Edinburgh
Butterworths
1994

| United Kingdom | Butterworth & Co (Publishers) Ltd, 4 Hill Street, EDINBURGH EH2 3JZ and Halsbury House, 35 Chancery Lane, LONDON WC2A 1EL |
| --- | --- |
| Australia | Butterworths, SYDNEY, MELBOURNE, BRISBANE, ADELAIDE, PERTH, CANBERRA and HOBART |
| Canada | Butterworths Canada Ltd, TORONTO and VANCOUVER |
| Ireland | Butterworth (Ireland) Ltd, DUBLIN |
| Malaysia | Malayan Law Journal Sdn Bhd, KUALA LUMPUR |
| New Zealand | Butterworths of New Zealand Ltd, WELLINGTON and AUCKLAND |
| Puerto Rico | Butterworth of Puerto Rico, Inc, SAN JUAN |
| Singapore | Butterworths Asia, SINGAPORE |
| South Africa | Butterworth Publishers (PTY) Ltd, DURBAN |
| USA | Butterworth Legal Publishers, CARLSBAD, California, and SALEM, New Hampshire |

A CIP Catalogue record for this book is available from the British Library.

ISBN 0 406 11543 5

Typeset by Phoenix Photosetting, Chatham, Kent
Printed and bound in Great Britain by
Thomson Litho Ltd, East Kilbride

# Preface

The aim of this short study is to examine, from a legal standpoint, the Scots law relating to confession evidence. Although it is primarily a book about the present state of the law, I have to a limited extent sought to examine the historical development where (it is hoped) this is helpful in understanding the present position. The tentative nature of many of the statements of the law is regrettable but unavoidable. However it is hoped that, if nothing else, this work will serve to provoke the deeper consideration of a fundamental and sometimes misunderstood area of the law of evidence.

I have made no attempt to address the 'psychological' aspects of confessions such as interrogation techniques or the increasingly recognised danger of interrogative suggestibility. Those interested in such matters should refer to published works by appropriately qualified authors.

This work draws on many sources, including personal experience of almost 20 years as a court practitioner. However, a particular debt is owed to that doyen of writing on the criminal law of Scotland, Sheriff G H Gordon. Sheriff Gordon's published writings on this subject were a major inspiration behind the doctoral thesis which I wrote for Glasgow University between 1988 and 1992 and from which this work is largely drawn. I am most grateful to Sheriff Gordon for setting out the trail for me to follow.

In common with most authors I owe much to those who have helped me in the production of this book. I am particularly grateful to the staff of Butterworths Law Publishers for their support and to Lord McCluskey for his warm encouragement. The debt which I owe to my wife Ann is beyond measure.

The views expressed in this work are wholly my own and I alone am responsible for the errors and omissions.

I have tried to state the law as at 31 December 1993.

David B Griffiths
*Glasgow*
*March 1994*

# Contents

# Contents

# Table of statutes

# TABLE OF STATUTES

# Table of cases

# List of abbreviations

**Law reports**

| | |
|---|---|
| AC | Law Reports, Appeal Cases (House of Lords and Privy Council) 1890– |
| Adam | Adam's Justiciary Reports 1894–1919 |
| All ER | All England Law Reports 1936– |
| Bell's Notes | Bell's Notes to Hume (4th edn) |
| Broun | Broun's Justiciary Reports 1842–45 |
| C & P | Carrington and Payne's Reports (Nisi Prius) 1823–41 |
| CLR | Commonwealth Law Reports (Australia) 1903– |
| Coup | Couper's Justiciary Reports 1868–85 |
| Crim App Rep | Criminal Appeal Reports 1908– |
| Crim LR | Criminal Law Review 1954– |
| Den CC | Denison's Crown Cases Reserved, 2 vols, 1844–52 |
| GWD | Green's Weekly Digest 1986– |
| Irv | Irvine's Justiciary Reports 1851–68 |
| J Shaw | J Shaw's Justiciary Reports 1848–51 |
| JC | Justiciary Cases 1917– |
| KB | Law Reports, King's Bench Division 1900–52 |
| Leach CC | Leach's Crown Cases, 2 vols, 1730–1814 |
| NI | Northern Ireland Law Reports 1925– |
| R (J) | Justiciary Cases in Rettie's Session Cases 1873–98 |
| RTR | Road Traffic Reports 1970– |
| SC (J) | Justiciary Cases in Session Cases 1907–16 |
| SCCR | Scottish Criminal Case Reports 1981– |
| SCCR Supp | Scottish Criminal Case Reports Supplement 1950–80 |
| SLT | Scots Law Times 1893–1908 (preceded by year and volume number), and 1909– (preceded by year) |
| SLT (Notes) | Notes of Recent Decisions in Scots Law Times 1946–1981 |
| Swin | Swinton's Justiciary Reports 1835–41 |

| WLR | Weekly Law Reports 1953– |
| White | White's Justiciary Reports 1885–93 |

## Journals

| Br J Crim | British Journal of Criminology |
| Camb LJ | Cambridge Law Journal |
| JLSS | Journal of the Law Society of Scotland |
| JR | Juridical Review |
| JSPTL | Journal of the Society of Public Teachers of the Law |
| LQR | Law Quarterly Review |
| MLR | Modern Law Review |
| NILQ | Northern Ireland Legal Quarterly |
| New LJ | New Law Journal |
| SCOLAG | Scottish Legal Action Group Bulletin |

## Textbooks

*Alison*, AJ: Principles and Practice of the Criminal Law of Scotland (1832/33)

*Burnett*, J: The Criminal Law of Scotland (1811)

*Dickson*, WG: The Law of Evidence of Scotland (2nd edn by PJH Grierson, 1887)

Gordon *Admissibility*: 'The Admissibility of Answers to Police Questioning in Scotland' in Glazebrook (ed) *Reshaping the Criminal Law* (1976)

*Hume*, David: Commentaries on the Law of Scotland Respecting Crimes (1844 edn by BR Bell)

*Lewis*, WJ: Manual of the Law of Evidence in Scotland (1925)

*Macdonald*, JHA: A Practical Treatise on the Criminal Law of Scotland (5th edn by J Walker and DJ Stevenson, 1948)

*Macphail*, ID: Evidence – a revised version of a research paper on the law of evidence in Scotland (1987)

*Renton and Brown*: Criminal Procedure According to the Law of Scotland (unless otherwise specified references are to 5th edn by GH Gordon, 1983)

*Walker and Walker*: The Law of Evidence in Scotland (1964)

*Wilkinson*, AB: The Scottish Law of Evidence (1986)

## Statutes

| | |
|---|---|
| 1975 Act | Criminal Procedure (Scotland) Act 1975 |
| 1980 Act | Criminal Justice (Scotland) Act 1980 |
| PACE | Police and Criminal Evidence Act 1984 |

# 1. Some basic issues

## INTRODUCTION

**1.01** Confession evidence is one of the commonest types of evidence tendered in the Scottish courts and it has a major place in the general law of criminal evidence. From the legal point of view, confessions come in many different forms. The least controversial is likely to be the plea of guilty freely tendered in open court. On the other hand there may be a lengthy series of 'special knowledge' admissions claimed to have been made in a police station or police car and subsequently vigorously denied by the alleged maker. The issue of what amounts to a 'confession' is discussed in detail later[1] but it should also be noted that even statements which are not *per se* incriminatory may be capable of having an incriminatory effect in an appropriate context and, on that basis, may come within the scope of confession evidence.

1 Para 1.22 below.

**1.02** Older texts including *Mackenzie*,[1] *Burnett*[2] and *Dickson*[3] divided confessions into 'judicial' and 'extra-judicial'. In this context the phrase 'judicial confession' was normally restricted to a 'confession on record', ie a plea of guilty which was accepted by the prosecutor. Confessions or admissions at judicial examination or other judicial proceedings were, on this basis, 'extra-judicial'. Such terminology is confusing and unhelpful and this study will follow the categorisation in the fourth edition of *Renton and Brown*[4] and treat all statements made in a judicial setting under the heading of 'judicial statements'. All other types of confession are treated as 'extra-judicial'.

1 *Works* II, 250.
2 *The Criminal Law of Scotland* p 578.
3 *The Law of Evidence in Scotland* p 209, §§ 286, 287.
4 *Criminal Procedure According to the Law of Scotland*.

**1.03** It is rare for there to be any controversy surrounding judicial statements and the making of an extra-judicial confession will often be followed by a plea of guilty.[1] However, when a case involving an extra-judicial confession proceeds to trial the confession evidence, particularly if coming from the police, is liable to be fiercely contested in court. When evidence of an extra-judicial confession is tendered there are, essentially, three basic issues: (1) was the confession actually made? (2) if the confession was made is it admissible in evidence? (3) if the confession is admissible what is its evidential effect?

1 For a summary of some English research on this point see M Zander 'The Right of Silence in the Police Station and the Caution' in Glazebrook (ed) *Reshaping the Criminal Law* p 344.

## THE NEED FOR AN ACCURATE RECORD

**1.04** It is probably self-evident that the determination of the three issues mentioned in the previous paragraph will be considerably simplified if there is available to the tribunal of fact a record of what was said which is demonstrably reliable. The introduction of a system of tape-recording of police interviews has gone a long way towards providing a reliable record of what was said in the course of the interview although neither tape-recording nor video-recording is an absolute guarantee of police probity, as recent English research has demonstrated.[1] Any form of electronic recording suffers from the major defect that the apparatus can only record what takes place within its range and is not proof against the informal preliminary chat or rehearsal. In addition, tape-recording has not been made a precondition of the admissibility of a confession as was recommended by the Thomson Committee.

In the absence of a tape-recording or some other demonstrably accurate record, the issue of whether the alleged statement was made (and the circumstances of its alleged making) will normally come to a question of credibility, a 'swearing contest' between the police and the accused. Curiously little attention has been paid by the Scottish courts to this aspect. It is distinctly worrying that the issue of the protection of the accused against the possibility of the fabrication of confession evidence has received no reported judicial consideration whatever in Scotland although most of the dangers were identified by *Dickson* over 100 years ago. While many judges, notably Lord Cooper, have animadverted on the dangers of the coercive pressure of custodial police interrogation, one will trawl the reports in vain for any Scottish equivalent of this forthright observation on the dangers of fabricated confessions by an Australian judge:

'It would be quite unrealistic to close one's eyes to the fact that for so long as there exists any danger that police officers may give perjured evidence there exists a danger that such evidence will involve the allegation that an oral confessional statement was made while an accused is held in custody without access to the safeguards and protection available to one who is not imprisoned.'[2]

While individual Scottish judges have occasionally voiced their personal concerns outwith the courtroom, such views have rarely, if ever, been expressed on the Scottish bench.[3]

1 M McConville 'Videotaping Interrogations' [1992] Crim LR 532 at 539.
2 *Clelland v The Queen* [1982] 151 CLR 1 at 25 per Deane J.
3 Eg Lord Justice-Clerk Ross *Herald* October 10, 1991; Lord McCluskey *Herald* November 2, 1993.

**1.05** Allegations of police 'verballing' are, of course, easy to make and, in fairness, it should be made clear right at the start of this study that there is no actual proof of widespread 'verballing' or other comparable misconduct by the Scottish police. Nevertheless, scandals in other jurisdictions involving fabricated or otherwise dubious confessions have moved the issue of the protection of the suspect much further up the agenda. Anecdotal evidence[1] also tends to suggest that juries are increasingly reluctant to convict on evidence which comes solely from police officers. While some may regard this as a good thing from the point of view of protecting the innocent against alleged police malpractice, it is hardly satisfactory when the police are, in fact, telling the whole truth. Although the point may not often be made, an unmerited acquittal based on a false perception of police mendacity is a miscarriage of justice. A demonstrably accurate record of what was said and the conditions under which it was said is a safeguard for both the suspect and the police themselves. Unless the issue of 'verballing', actual or perceived, is tackled there is probably little point in worrying about issues such as fairness or corroboration. Any police officer who is prepared to fabricate a confession, or touch up a genuine one to make it more convincing, is likely to be equally prepared to fabricate corroboration or otherwise bend the facts and, as will be seen later in the context of sufficiency, the modern 'special knowledge' rule can sometimes operate in a way which almost invites malpractice by a dishonest policeman.

1 See eg Murray Ritchie *Herald* June 25, 1990.

## THE HISTORICAL AND CONTINUING INFLUENCE OF SCOTS COMMON LAW

**1.06**   While certain statutes make individual rules for particular circumstances, the Scots law of evidence remains overwhelmingly a matter of common law and this is very much the case in relation to confession evidence Scots law has largely avoided the detailed statutory regulation imposed in England and Wales by the Police and Criminal Evidence Act 1984 and still depends on law built up case by case by the judges over a period of some one and a half centuries. In any system of this nature the individual circumstances of the particular case will be important to the eventual decision which is also likely to be affected, to an extent, by the attitude and temperament of the contemporary judiciary. Scottish cases concerning confession evidence cannot generally be separated from their particular facts or their historical background.

**1.07**   We know from *Hume*[1] that Scots law has always admitted spontaneous voluntary extra-judicial statements by accused persons made without questioning. However, historically the right to interrogate a prisoner lay exclusively with the magistrate (normally the sheriff) at the declaration, although this procedure was to decline to the point of extinction following the passing of the Criminal Evidence Act 1898 and the granting to the accused of the right to give evidence on his own behalf. With the establishment of organised police forces, essentially a phenomenon of the nineteenth century, the police began to assume the major responsibility for the detection and apprehension of suspects. Along with this went the assumption by the police of a more positive role in the questioning of suspects. Such activities were, and remain, largely unregulated by statute and at a very early stage the courts became concerned to protect suspects against possible police abuse and particularly the possibility of the police applying unfair pressure to induce a confession. In addition the courts continued for many years to fight a rearguard action against what they regarded as the usurpation of their function by the upstart police.[2] Indeed, a remarkable example of the judiciary's reluctance to acknowledge reality can be found as late as 1961 when one judge ruled inadmissible an apparently unexceptionable voluntary statement to the police because the prisoner had not been taken before a magistrate.[3] Even more remarkably, in an essay published in 1966 Lord Kilbrandon was prepared to argue that it was law of Scotland that 'if a person in custody who has been charged with a crime makes a statement about that crime that statement will not be allowed in evidence unless it has been emitted before a magistrate in due course of law'.[4] This can best be described as wishful thinking, the judicial declaration having largely been an empty shell since the turn of the century, but nevertheless it is an important insight into the extreme historical conservatism of certain members of the Scottish judiciary.

1 *Commentaries* II, 333.
2 Eg *Hodgson v Macpherson* 1913 SC (J) 69 at 74.
3 D B Smith 'A Note on Judicial Examination' 1961 SLT (News) 179.
4 J A Coutts (ed) *The Accused* p 65.

**1.08** One of the most important results of the reliance on common law has been the ability of the Scottish judges to bring about material alterations if not in the law itself then certainly in the way in which it has been applied. When the issue of police interrogation first began to come before the courts, the tendency was to regard the matter as one of competency but since the late nineteenth century 'fairness' has been the accepted test. The fairness test itself has changed in nature over the years. At first 'fairness' meant fairness to the accused and the determination of the issue was a matter for the judge. Essentially the question was one of judicial discretion. From the late 1920s until the early 1950s the Scottish judiciary went through what can only be described as an 'anti police' phase culminating in the celebrated case of *Chalmers v HM Advocate*.[1] At this time there was a definite tendency towards a firm exclusionary rule, which would have rendered inadmissible any confession obtained by questioning in the police station, although this was never in fact achieved. *Chalmers* also made a major procedural change with the introduction of the 'trial within a trial' as the approved means of determining the question of fairness. However, within a very short space of time the whole climate had changed and by the late 1960s the fairness test had become bilateral. The courts were now to consider fairness to the public and to seek to balance the rights of the individual against the need to avoid 'hamstringing the police with a series of academic vetoes which ignore the realities and practicalities of the situation and discount completely the public interest'.[2] Along with this has come the view that the determination of fairness is essentially a matter for the jury.

1 1954 JC 66.
2 *Miln v Cullen* 1967 JC 21.

**1.09** This flexibility of approach is characteristic of the Scottish approach to the criminal law generally which tends to avoid theoretical distinction and proceed on a pragmatic, common sense basis. While this undoubtedly enables the law to develop to meet changing circumstances it has the disadvantage that it tends to produce 'ad hoc' results and may on occasion lead to the law being difficult to predict. Professor Gerard Maher has argued that:

'One problem about this state of affairs is that it makes the law unknowable, for everything will depend on how judges in particular cases weigh the conflicting rights and interests involved, and although each case may well have one right answer which the balancing test will provide and which the judges will usually arrive at, this cannot easily be known in advance. Accordingly the use of the balance as part of the judicial technique puts a major hole in the desideratum of legality, that laws be clear and knowable.'[1]

1 'Balancing Rights and Interests in the Criminal Process' in Duff and Simmonds (eds) *Philosophy and the Criminal Law*.

**1.10** While this criticism is undoubtedly cogent, the problem is that the only alternatives to judicial discretion are either a firm exclusionary rule, which is alien to the Scottish tradition, or a rule that all confessions are admissible irrespective of the means by which they have been procured, which is clearly unacceptable. Even in England where confession evidence is now regulated in great detail by the Police and Criminal Evidence Act 1984 and its associated codes of practice it has been necessary to make explicit statutory provision in section 78(1) of the Act for the courts to retain a generalised discretion to exclude evidence in the interests of fairness. Judicial discretion will clearly continue to play a major part in determining the admissibility of confession evidence in Scotland and each case will, to an extent, depend on its own infinitely variable facts, as Lord Justice-General Emslie made clear in *Lord Advocate's Reference (No 1 of 1983)*:

'In each case . . . it will be necessary to consider the whole relevant circumstances in order to discover whether or not there has been unfairness on the part of the police resulting in the extraction from the suspect of the answers in question. Unfairness may take many forms but if answers are to be excluded they must be seen to have been extracted by unfair means which place cross-examination, pressure and deception in close company.'[1]

1 1984 JC 52, 1984 SCCR 62, 1984 SLT 337.

## THE RIGHT TO SILENCE

**1.11** In the Scottish context the 'right to silence' embraces the right of the accused not to testify at his trial and the right of the suspect to refuse to answer police questions without incurring adverse consequences such as a penal sanction, a presumption of guilt or adverse comment at the trial. The right to silence can be viewed as an aspect of the presumption of innocence – it helps to ensure that the prosecution cannot discharge the burden of proof by requiring the suspect to provide evidence against himself. The phrases 'right to silence' and 'privilege against self-incrimination' are sometimes incorrectly regarded as synonymous. While the right to silence is related to the privilege against self-incrimination, the latter privilege, sometimes referred to by the Latin maxim *nemo tenetur jurare in suam turpitudinem*, is wider in scope and entitles any witness, not necessarily an accused person, to refuse to answer a question if the true answer would be likely to lead to his conviction for a crime.

**1.12** In Scots law, as in other systems, many of the problems inherent in confession evidence stem from a tension between the right of silence, particularly as it applies in relation to police questioning, and the need of the police or other questioner to obtain information from the suspect. There has, for many years, been a vigorous debate in England on whether the right to silence should be modified or possibly even abolished altogether.[1] The English debate can be traced back to the time of Jeremy Bentham and his celebrated observation that:

'If criminals of every class had assembled, and framed a system after their own minds, is not this rule the very first which they would have established for their security? Innocence never takes advantage of it. Innocence claims the right of speaking, as guilt invokes the privilege of silence.'[2]

Some of the most influential figures in English law, notably Professors Glanville Williams and Sir Rupert Cross, have been among the most vigorous opponents of the right to silence, Cross having on one occasion described it as a 'sacred cow'.[3] However, it has not generally been suggested that it should become a criminal offence to refuse to answer police questions or refuse to testify in court but the English debate has centred on whether silence should be the subject of adverse comment in court, or possibly even attract a presumption of guilt. Although research has suggested that the right to silence is by no means the problem which certain police officers believe,[4] as this book goes to print the Criminal Justice and Public Order Bill presently before Parliament looks likely to end the right to silence as it has been known in England and Wales. If enacted, this measure will allow the court to draw adverse inferences from silence in the face of police questioning and will require the court to call on the accused to give evidence and if he refuses the court may, once again, draw adverse inferences.

1 See S Greer 'The Right to Silence: a Review of the Current Debate' (1990) 53 MLR 709.
2 *Treatise on Evidence* p 241.
3 (1970) 11 JSPTL 66.
4 Eg B Mitchell 'Confessions and Police Interrogation of Suspects' [1983] Crim LR 596; S Greer, note 1, above; J Baldwin 'Police Interview Techniques' (1993) 33 Br J Crim 325; Royal Commission on Criminal Justice Research Study No 10 (HMSO, 1993).

**1.13** In Scotland the right to silence first appears to have been asserted in the Claim of Right which stated that 'The forceing the leidges to Depone against themselves in capitall Crymes however the punishment be restricted is Contrary to law'. The right to silence has never been such a controversial issue in Scotland as it has in England. The Thomson Committee contented itself with the observation that a system in which there was a duty to provide answers to the police would be too heavily weighted against the suspect.[1] Nevertheless, even though the Scottish courts have not generally relied on the right to silence as a factor in judicial decision making, preferring instead to concentrate on the question of fairness, the right does exist in Scotland and its influence is extensive.

1 Departmental Committee on Criminal Procedure in Scotland (Second Report) (1975, Cmnd 6218) para 7.05.

**1.14** Historically in Scotland, as in England, the accused was not competent to testify in his own defence. Silence was enforced on him rather than being a right which he could waive or exercise as he saw fit. In England Bentham suggested that this situation arose because of a reaction against the detested Courts of Star Chamber and High Commission which had interrogated on oath anyone unfortunate enough to stand trial before them. The reason for the origin of the parallel position in Scotland is unclear although at one time no evidence at all contrary to the libel was admitted. When this practice was modified is uncertain but according to *Hume*[1] it had definitely changed by the middle of the eighteenth century. Notwithstanding this, the accused was not to obtain the right to give evidence for a further century and a half. The Scottish accused was probably marginally better off than his English counterpart since in most Scottish cases a declaration would have been taken which would have allowed the accused to put his story on record. Nevertheless although the declaration was admissible against the accused, he could not found on it as evidence in his favour.[2] Moreover, the declaration could only be read to the trial court with the consent of the Crown which might be withheld without justification as certainly happened in the case of *Elizabeth Kennedy or Potts*[3] the report of which makes reference to another case, *Margaret Wright*, in the same sitting where consent to the reading of the declaration was refused by the same Advocate Depute.

1 II, 297.
2 *Alison* II, 555.
3 (1842) 1 Broun 497.

**1.15** When section 1 of the Criminal Evidence Act 1898 (now sections 141 and 346 of the Criminal Procedure (Scotland) Act 1975) finally rectified the situation and made the accused a competent witness for the defence, provisions were written into the statute to ensure that he could only be called on his own application and also to forbid the prosecution from commenting on his failure to give evidence. The statute therefore placed emphasis on competence rather than compellability. It did, however, provide that if the accused elects to give evidence he becomes liable to cross-examination even if that tends to incriminate him as to the offence charged. Despite the fact that the statute unequivocally prohibits the prosecution from making adverse comment on the accused's silence, in none of the reported Scottish decisions on this issue has the conviction actually been overturned.[1] Despite the fact that the High Court is obviously reluctant to overturn a conviction on this ground, it must nevertheless remain a possibility, particularly in a jury trial, if the trial judge does not deal adequately with the point in his charge to the jury.[2]

1 *Ross v Boyd* (1903) 4 Adam 184; *McHugh v HM Advocate* 1978 JC 12; *Upton v HM Advocate* 1986 SCCR 188.
2 See P W F 'The Right to Silence' 1987 SLT 17.

**1.16** The statute makes no explicit provision for the possibility of adverse comment by the judge. Despite some early hesitancy it is now settled law in Scotland that the trial judge is entitled in appropriate circumstances to comment on the failure of the accused to give evidence and to draw that failure to the attention of the jury. However this is a particularly delicate area and the judge will require to be careful to ensure that the jury does not receive an erroneous impression that silence is evidence against the accused.[1]

1 *Brown v Macpherson* 1918 JC 3; *Scott (A T) v HM Advocate* 1946 JC 90; *Knowles v HM Advocate* 1975 JC 6; *Stewart v HM Advocate* 1980 SLT 245. See also *Dorrens v HM Advocate* 1983 SCCR 407.

**1.17** In principle the revived judicial examination procedure under sections 20, 20A and 20B of the 1975 Act derogates from an accused's right to silence.[1] However, it does so only indirectly and has no effect on the suspect's right not to talk to the police or the accused's right not to testify at his trial. The procedure gives the prosecutor a right to question the accused, in front of the sheriff, on matters averred in the charge and on any extra-judicial confession. The statute places stringent limits on the prosecutor's questioning, which is to be directed towards obtaining particulars of the accused's defence rather than attempting to incriminate him. However, it also provides that if the accused declines to answer questions at examination but then at the trial either gives or leads evidence of something which could appropriately have been stated at the examination, adverse comment may be made by the judge, the prosecutor or a co-accused. Such comment may be made even where the accused has declined to answer on legal advice.[2] Nevertheless, in practice the impact of judicial examination on the right to silence of the majority of accused has been minimal.[3] Although the accused retains his historic right to emit a declaration, this is infrequent and unless the accused forces the issue by emitting a declaration, it is a matter entirely within the discretion of the prosecution whether an examination is held. In many cases none will take place. In addition it is clear from *Walker v HM Advocate*[4] that there is no possibility of adverse comment unless the accused gives or leads evidence at the trial; so an accused who is consistent throughout, saying nothing at examination and not giving evidence at his trial, has nothing to fear from judicial examination.

1 A detailed description of the procedure is outwith the scope of this work and the reader is referred to *Renton and Brown* para 5–58 ff.
2 *Alexander v HM Advocate* 1988 SCCR 542; *McEwan v HM Advocate* 1990 SCCR 401; cf *McGhee v HM Advocate* 1991 SCCR 510.
3 See I D Macphail 'Safeguards in the Scottish Criminal Justice System' [1992] Crim LR 144, especially at 147.
4 1985 SCCR 150.

**1.18** The right to silence at the stage of police interview is not a statutory right but it arises from the right to silence at the trial. This was explained by Lord Justic-General Cooper in *Chalmers v HM Advocate*:

'If it were competent for the police at their own hand to subject the accused to interrogation and cross-examination and to adduce evidence of what he said, the prosecution would, in effect, be making the accused a compellable witness, and laying before the jury, at second hand, evidence which could not be adduced at first hand even subject to all the precautions which are available for the protection of the accused at a criminal trial.'[1]

1 1954 JC 66 at 79.

**1.19** A right is, of course, only meaningful if the person concerned is aware that he possesses it and the most visible effect of the right to silence is the requirement on the police to caution a suspect before questioning him. As will be discussed later, the requirement to caution does not arise where the police or other investigator has a specific power to require information. However, statutory exceptions apart, no offence is committed by any person who refuses to talk to the police.

**1.20** Parliament may modify or even abolish the right to silence at any or all stages of the criminal process. In Britain this has been haphazard but the tendency has been to abrogate the right at the investigative stage rather than the trial. For the time being at least, the right to silence in court is absolute, subject only to the possibility of adverse judicial comment.[1] On the other hand at the earlier stages the right to silence is by no means absolute. Several statutes have made substantial inroads into it. Probably the best known example of this is the right of the police now contained in section 172(2) of the Road Traffic Act 1988 to require, under sanction of a criminal charge, information as to the identity of the driver of a motor vehicle who is alleged to be guilty of an offence. Another well known example is section 2 of the Criminal Justice Act 1987 which gives the Director of the Serious Fraud Office extensive powers to require information. Such provisions will be strictly construed by the courts.[2]

1 Para 1.16 above.
2 Paras 2.99–2.106 below.

## THE EVIDENTIAL EFFECT OF SILENCE

**1.21** Silence when questioned by the police, in the early stage of an inquiry, may, in certain very limited circumstances, be regarded as a 'criminative circumstance' in the doctrine of recent possession of stolen property.[1] Apart from this, and the special circumstance of the 'implied confession',[2] silence is not evidence against the accused.[3] In *Robertson v Maxwell*[4] Lord Justice-General Cooper made it clear that 'no legitimate inference in favour of a prosecutor can be drawn from the fact that a person, when charged with crime, either says nothing or says that he has nothing to say. He is entitled to reserve his defence and it is usually wise to do so'. This point was re-emphasised in *Wightman v HM Advocate*[5] where the conviction was quashed because the sheriff-substitute had misdirected the jury that failure to reply to caution and charge and failure to give evidence in court could constitute criminative circumstances in regard to possession of stolen property. More recently it was held in *White v HM Advocate*[6] that 'I'm saying nothing about it' could not be construed as indicating knowledge of the presence of controlled drugs.

1 See *Fox v Patterson* 1948 JC 104; G H Gordon 'The Burden of Proof on the Accused' 1968 SLT (News) 29.
2 Paras 3.01–3.06 below.
3 Realistically, it has to be acknowledged that while it would not be 'legitimate', such silence could suggest to a jury that a story which only appears for the first time at a late stage is untrue. It is difficult to draw a distinction between factors pointing to the accused's incredibility and factors pointing to his guilt.
4 1951 SLT 46.

## DEFINITION OF CONFESSION

**1.22** In most cases the question of whether the accused's words amount to a 'confession' is a straightforward issue of fact. There is normally little difficulty in relation to judicial confessions but in relation to extra-judicial confessions the matter is sometimes less clearcut. Scotland lacks the statutory definition of a confession which section 82(1) of the Police and Criminal Evidence Act 1984 has provided in England: 'Any statement wholly or partly adverse to the person who made it . . . whether made in words or otherwise'. Nevertheless, even the briefest glance at the Scottish cases shows that in Scotland the term 'confession' obviously embraces much more than the 'Yes I murdered my wife' type of statement. The only statutory definition in Scotland is in section 20A(1)(b) of the Criminal Procedure (Scotland) Act 1975 which entitles the prosecutor to question the accused at judicial examination on 'an extrajudicial confession (whether or not a full admission)', the obvious implication being that something falling short of a full admission of guilt may nevertheless amount to a 'confession' at least for the purpose of judicial examination. In *McKenzie v HM Advocate*[1] the statutory phrase was interpreted to mean 'that the definition of "confession" must be that the statement is clearly susceptible of being regarded as an incriminating statement'.

1 1982 SCCR 545.

**1.23** While the words used by the suspect are of major importance, it is self-evident that no statement can be isolated from the context in which it is made. The manner in which a statement is made may also be vitally important – 'Yes, sure, I did it' could be an unequivocal admission or a sarcastic denial depending on the tone of voice used which, of course, emphasises once again the need for an accurate record capable of allowing the court to hear exactly what was said and how. It also follows that a statement which is *ex facie* innocent or even exculpatory, may become at least partly incriminatory in an appropriate context. Statements such as 'Just my luck, I knew I'd get picked out', 'I wisnae the driver' or 'You don't know where it happened, you've got no proof' have incriminatory potential in an appropriate context. The clearest example of this point is *Moran v HM Advocate*[1] where the accused gave the police detailed information about a murder which he claimed to have got from a named individual. Police inquiries established that the individual concerned had been in custody at the time of the murder and the Crown successfully founded on the accused's statements as showing 'special knowledge' of the murder. The High Court held that the statements had been correctly put to the accused at judicial examination and correctly admitted in evidence at the trial. *Moran* was described as

'an outstanding example of a situation where it could only properly be decided whether an alleged extrajudicial statement made by the accused could properly be regarded as an admission or partial admission . . . in the light of other evidence.'

In addition, in *Khan v HM Advocate*,[2] a mixed statement case, the High Court took the view that the test of whether a statement was part incriminatory was whether a reasonable jury would be entitled so to regard it in the knowledge of all the facts about the case. In modern Scots law a statement can thus amount to a 'confession' when it can reasonably be regarded as incriminatory in its context. On this basis, the response 'I'm sorry' made by an accused when charged with theft by shoplifting has been held, in the context of the other evidence, to be capable of meaning that the accused was impliedly admitting that she had committed the offence.[3]

1 1990 SCCR 40.
2 1992 SCCR 146.
3 *Lauchlan v Hamilton* 1993 SCCR 1057.


## NON-VERBAL CONFESSIONS

**1.24**  We have seen that the English definition acknowledges that a confession need not necessarily be a verbal statement. Conduct may sometimes be equivalent to words and it would seem to be in accordance with principle for conduct of an incriminating nature to be subject to the same rules of law as verbal confessions. There are some easy examples. A nod of the head may well be equivalent to a verbal 'Yes'. The taking of the police to the spot where a body is buried or some other important evidence is found is at least as incriminating as a detailed verbal confession. One graphic example is the English case of *R v Voisin*.[1] In this case the headless and handless body of a woman had been found in a parcel along with a piece of paper with the singular phrase 'Bladie Belgiam' written on it. Voisin was seen by the police and asked to account for his movements at the relevant time. He made a voluntary statement without being cautioned and then one of the policemen asked him if he would mind writing the words

'Bloody Belgian'. Voisin replied 'Not at all' and promptly signed his own death warrant by writing 'Bladie Belgiam'.

1 [1918] 1 KB 531.

**1.25**  In Scotland *Chalmers v HM Advocate*[1] is the only reported case to deal explicitly with the admissibility of incriminatory conduct and in that case it was held that the law relating to fairness was applicable to incriminatory actions. In *Chalmers* the conduct in question, taking the police to a field where the deceased's purse was found, was self-evidently incriminatory and no issue arose as to whether there was any other possible explanation. However, difficult questions could arise if the conduct was capable of bearing either an innocent or an incriminatory interpretation, for example if the suspect bursts into tears or runs off. Such conduct would be most unlikely to be intended as an admission of guilt by the individual concerned but could well be taken as such by a perfectly reasonable layman. There is no modern law either north or south of the Border dealing squarely with this question. In *McGougan v HM Advocate*[2] there was evidence that the accused, when confronted by the parents of a child he was alleged to have assaulted, was seen to hang his head and later he allegedly attempted to throw himself from a window. The way matters developed, the point at issue was not whether these actions were incriminatory in themselves but whether they could corroborate other admissions made by the accused. The distinction may be of little substance, but the Crown eventually conceded that the actions could not be used as corroboration. Although no explanation was given for the concession, it could well have been made on the basis that both the admissions and the conduct originated from the same source, the accused, and therefore could not corroborate each other.

1 1954 JC 66.
2 1991 SCCR 49.

**1.26**  The point, however, is that *McGougan* did not decide whether such actions could be regarded as incriminatory and the High Court has yet to express any clear view on the extent to which actions of this sort can be held equivalent to a verbal confession. It is submitted that *Dickson*[1] was correct when he observed under reference to several old English authorities that 'Fear or attempts at flight on the part of one directly charged with a serious crime are of little weight as indications of guilt', a statement which has never been contradicted or doubted in any reported case.

1 Page 73, § 91.

# THE CONFESSION AS HEARSAY EVIDENCE

**1.27**  We know from *Hume*[1] that evidence of what an accused person said against his interest to another witness has always been *prima facie* admissible in Scotland and the extra-judicial confession constitutes one of the most commonly encountered exceptions to the rule of Scots criminal law that hearsay is inadmissible as evidence of the truth of what is asserted – 'Any assertion other than one made by a person while giving oral evidence in the proceedings is inadmissible as evidence of any fact asserted'.[2] The exception to the rule against hearsay is normally justified on the basis that what someone says to his prejudice is likely to be true and therefore free from the disadvantage of unreliability which often attaches to hearsay evidence.[3] As *Dickson*[4] puts it, 'Extrajudicial confessions, whether made orally or in writing, are admissible in criminal cases, and for the manifest reason that they are far more likely to be true than false'.

1  II, 333.
2  *Morrison v HM Advocate* 1990 SCCR 235 at 247.
3  Wilkinson *The Scottish Law of Evidence* p 41.
4  Page 240, § 343.

# ADMISSIBILITY AND RELEVANCY – GENERAL ISSUES

**1.28**  To be admissible evidence must satisfy two requirements – it must be relevant and it must conform to the peremptory rules of evidence. Relevancy depends on the existence of some sort of logical relationship between the evidence and the subject matter of the case.

'Irrelevant evidence is never admissible, but even relevant evidence may be made inadmissible by one of the peremptory rules which the law prescribes. These rules, which are mainly negative in character, are imposed by the law for reasons of policy. They spring from the knowledge that the discovery of the truth by a human tribunal from what is said by human witnesses is a difficult task, and they attempt to limit the evil consequences of error by excluding certain kinds of evidence as being insufficiently reliable, or too remote, or as creating the possibility of unfairness or confusion.'[1]

1  Walker and Walker *The Law of Evidence in Scotland* p 1.

**1.29**  Issues of relevancy seldom arise in relation to confession evidence – clearly a statement by the accused implicating himself in the offence with which he is charged is in the highest degree relevant to the proof of the case against him. The main focus in regard to admissibility of confession evidence is on the 'peremptory rule' which excludes a wrongfully obtained confession. Issues of admissibility almost always relate to the circumstances under which the statement in question came to be made and it has been pointed out that in Scottish terms what has normally been in issue has been not so much the truth of the accused's statements as the propriety of the circumstances in which they were made. Statements improperly obtained are not evidence however reliable and obviously true. According to the Second Report of the Thomson Committee[1] such statements are excluded by the courts because 'an exclusionary rule is the only effective weapon possessed by the courts to control police interrogation'.

1 Para 7.02.

**1.30** Scots law has never had anything akin to the Judges Rules and the Scottish courts have been extremely reluctant to articulate any policy or rationale behind their attitude to the admission of confessions although opinions in many of the cases naturally dwell on the improper conduct of the police. It is arguable that as a matter of strict law the courts have nothing to do with how the police conduct their affairs, the only question for the courts being whether a particular piece of evidence is admissible. However, the conduct of the police is clearly a matter of the highest public interest and the exclusion of evidence by the courts is, as the Thomson Committee acknowledged, one of the few ways in which society can indicate to the police that their conduct has gone beyond what is acceptable. Nevertheless, it is very difficult to establish exactly why the Scottish courts have adopted the current attitude towards confessions. It has been suggested that the true reason for the fairness test is that it is important to be as certain as possible that the confession is true:

'This is normally achieved by ensuring that it is voluntary, which is the principal reason for the fairness test. Thus, goes the argument, a confession which is fairly obtained is likely to be voluntary, and therefore likely to be true. The confession which is unfairly obtained may still be true, but it is contrary to public policy, and unsafe, to rely on any confession so obtained.'[1]

1 D Field *The Law of Evidence in Scotland* p 298.

## THE CONFESSION AS CIRCUMSTANTIAL EVIDENCE

**1.31** It is arguable whether modern law continues to regard an extra-judicial confession as a piece of circumstantial evidence or a separate class of evidence in its own right. Returning yet again to *Hume*,[1] it is clear that he regarded the extra-judicial confession as circumstantial evidence:

'Indeed, a verbal confession is often so interwoven with the other facts and circumstances in the case, that it cannot without violence be separated from them; nor the witnesses give their evidence intelligibly, or with due connection, without relating this part of the story also. In a case of theft, if on being seized with the stolen goods upon him, the thief instantly confess his crime, and offer back the goods, or tempt the owner with a bribe to let him go; or in a case of murder, if the killer be taken red-hand, and brought into the presence of the dying man, and there lament his rashness, and ask forgiveness of his victim: Such incidents are not mere words of acknowledgment; they are links in the chain of circumstances, and equally bear evidence against the pannel, as the blood on his clothes, or the goods found concealed on his person.'

The rule that no-one may be convicted solely on the evidence of an extra-judicial confession[2] is certainly consistent with the view that such a confession is an item of circumstantial evidence, as is the rule that the making of a confession (which is not of the 'special knowledge' variety) is sufficiently proved by a single witness.[3] However, against this view is the rule that a confession is not corroborated by being repeated, even in different terms to different witnesses.[4] It is thought that the better view is that under modern conditions the extra-judicial confession is in a special category of its own and subject to its own particular rules although in certain circumstances the principles of circumstantial evidence continue to be relevant.

1 II, 333.
2 Para 5.33 ff below.
3 *Mills v HM Advocate* 1935 JC 77; *Innes v HM Advocate* 1955 SLT (Notes) 69.
4 *Bainbridge v Scott* 1988 SLT 871.

# THE ACCUSED'S OWN ACTS

**1.32**   The present study is primarily concerned with confessions and admissions as evidence of the accused's own acts and based on the accused's own knowledge. It is a general rule that a confession made by accused A and incriminating accused B is not admissible as evidence against B, since it is, in an issue concerning B, hearsay evidence.[1] The so-called 'implied confession' where A makes his statement in B's hearing, which might at first sight appear to be an exception to this principle, is not truly so since the evidence against B is his reaction to A's statement and the statement is admissible only for the purpose of explaining B's reaction.[2] The statement in *Annan v Bain and Hamill*[3] that the confession of one accused may be used to corroborate the confession of another is, with respect, manifestly incorrect and was rightly described by Sheriff Gordon as 'contrary to authority and principle'.

1 Macdonald *The Criminal Law of Scotland* (5th edn) p 315; *McIntosh v HM Advocate* 1986 SCCR 496.
2 Para 3.01 below.
3 1986 SCCR 60.

**1.33** Although there is no Scottish authority directly in point it is thought that the Scottish courts would follow the English view that admissions which are not based on the accused's personal knowledge are not admissible to prove the acts of other persons. It was said in the English case of *Surujpaul v R*[1] that:

'A voluntary statement made by an accused person is admissible as a "confession". He can confess as to his own acts, knowledge or intentions, but he cannot "confess" as to the acts of other persons which he has not seen and of which he can only have knowledge by hearsay. A failure by the prosecution to prove an essential element in the offence cannot be cured by an "admission" of this nature.'

In other words, if A says, 'B told me he had stolen the goods', that statement would clearly be admissible against A himself if he were on trial for reset, since it establishes guilty knowledge. However, such a statement would not prove that the goods were in fact stolen and the Crown would require to prove this by other evidence apart from A's statement.

1 [1958] 1 WLR 1050.

# 2. The admissibility of confession evidence

## JUDICIAL STATEMENTS

### Guilty plea

**2.01** *Burnett*[1] declares that 'A confession by a prisoner in open court, and in presence of the assize is of all sorts of evidence the best and most convincing; it being an attestation of guilt, *sua ipsis voce et indicio*'.

1 *The Criminal Law of Scotland* p 576.

**2.02** Historically, Scottish procedure prior to 1828 required a plea of guilty by the pannel to be referred to a jury, who had to return a verdict, before the court could proceed to sentence. The court had to be sure that the confession was truly voluntary and made without the influence of hope or fear. *Burnett*, echoing *Mackenzie*, states:

'For, as confessions, even in open court, may be the effect of undue means antecedently used; – may arise from a derangement of intellect and *"rather out of weariness of life, than a consciousness of guilt"*; and as the law has laid great weight upon the way and manner in which a confession is elicited, measuring exactly the degree of constancy of fear appearing in the pannel, as well as considering the motives by which he may be induced to confess; and joined to all these, as confessions may be qualified, and in circumstances annexed to them, the import of which may admit of doubt, it has been deemed wiser to entrust the cognizance of this sort of proof, as well as of every other, to a jury, leaving it to them to judge of it, and to inquire, if they see needful, into the situation of the prisoner, his state of mind at the time, and the circumstances or motives which may have induced him to confess.'[1]

1 *Burnett* pp 576–577.

**2.03** The Circuit Courts (Scotland) Act 1828 made it unnecessary, although not incompetent, to refer a plea of guilty to a jury and in modern Scottish practice a plea of guilty, whether 'as libelled' or in some modified form which is accepted by the prosecutor, will normally be accepted without any inquiry by the court, no considerations of admissibility normally arising. Nevertheless, even in modern solemn procedure section 103(1) of the Criminal Procedure (Scotland) Act 1975 still requires the accused to attest the voluntariness of his confession by signing a copy of the plea, which must be countersigned by the judge. In summary procedure an accused who is present in court is required to tender his plea personally unless he is incapable of doing so.[1]

1 Act of Adjournal (Consolidation) 1988, r 119(1) and (2).

**2.04** It is at least arguable that in Scottish procedure the court has no *locus* to inquire into the background to a plea of guilty since the prosecutor is 'master of the instance' and it is for the Crown to decide whether a particular plea is to be accepted. In particular if the Crown elects to accept a plea of guilty to a restricted charge, the court cannot insist on the original charge going to trial nor, it is submitted, could either the prosecutor or those acting for the accused be required to justify their actions to the court.[1]

1 On the Scottish form of plea bargaining see A V Sheehan *Criminal Procedure* paras 3.32–3.36.

## Refusal of guilty plea

**2.05** The prosecutor is not obliged to accept a plea of guilty in either solemn or summary procedure.[1] The leading authority on this subject is *Strathearn v Sloan*[2] in which the High Court made it clear that where a plea of guilty is tendered and not accepted it must under no circumstances be used against the accused and where the trial is on indictment it must not be disclosed to the jury. In addition, if the accused, notwithstanding his plea of guilty, chooses to enter the witness box, he must have entire freedom to give evidence contrary to the plea of guilty which the prosecutor has declined to accept.[3] *Strathearn v Sloan* was decided at the time when there were two diets in all solemn cases and in *Strathearn* Lord Aitchison laid down that where the plea was tendered and refused at the first diet the accused should not be called upon to plead at the second diet unless the Crown had, in the meantime, decided to accept the plea of guilty. The abolition of the mandatory first diet following on the Criminal Justice (Scotland) Act 1980 means that the first time the accused is called upon to plead is likely to be in front of a roomful of unempannelled jurors and it is difficult to see how it is possible to avoid either the accused's plea or the Crown's refusal of it coming to their attention.

1 *David Peter and John Smith* (1840) 2 Swin 492; *Strathearn v Sloan* 1937 JC 76. See also 'An Aspect of Criminal Procedure' (1956) 72 SLR 221.

2  1937 JC 76.
3  See also *Cochran v Ferguson* (1882) 5 Coup 169; *Brown v Macpherson* 1918 JC 3.


*Withdrawal of guilty plea*

**2.06**  Accused persons sometimes have second thoughts about the wisdom of having pled guilty, particularly if legal advice is only obtained after the guilty plea has been tendered. Provided conviction and sentence have not yet followed, it is a matter for the discretion of the court whether to allow leave for a plea of guilty to be withdrawn although theoretically the accused will require to show trickery, coercion or genuine misunderstanding.[1] In summary procedure leave will tend to be allowed if there is *prima facie* justification, particularly if the prosecution does not object. However, leave is unlikely to be allowed if the accused has tendered his plea personally or if the plea has been tendered with legal advice.[2] Once conviction has followed the only way for an accused to withdraw a plea of guilty is by a Bill of Suspension to the High Court.[3]

1  Renton and Brown *Criminal Procedure According to the Law of Scotland* paras 14–29, 16–44; *Smith v Carmichael* 1987 SCCR 735.
2  *Black v Lockhart* 1992 GWD 38–2231; *MacGregor v MacNeill* 1975 JC 57; *Pirie v McNaughtan* 1991 SCCR 483.
3  *MacGregor v MacNeill* above; cf *McConnachie v Scott* 1988 SLT 480.


**2.07**  In solemn procedure it has been held competent to withdraw a plea in the sheriff court, but this may only be done where the plea has been tendered under some real error or misconception or in circumstances clearly prejudicial to the accused. When the charge has been read over to the accused who has confirmed his plea of guilty, the only reasonable conclusion is that the accused willingly accepts the allegations and the court will not allow the plea to be changed.[1] It is unclear whether the principle of *Strathearn v Sloan*[2] which prevents the prosecutor from founding on a plea of guilty which he has refused also applies in the situation where the accused tenders a plea which is later allowed to be withdrawn. One leading authority[3] considers that it does but the withdrawal of a plea in solemn procedure is a very rare occurrence and there is no reported decision on the point.

1  *Healy v HM Advocate* 1990 SCCR 110; cf *Evans, Petitioner* 1991 SCCR 160. See also *Renton and Brown* para 8-09.
2  1937 JC 76.
3  Macphail *Evidence* § 2.25.

*Plea of guilty as evidence in other charges*

**2.08** Following *Walsh v HM Advocate*,[1] in solemn procedure no reference may be made in the course of a trial to any charge on the indictment to which the accused has pleaded guilty, since such a charge is no longer before the jury. However, in summary procedure *McColl v Skeen*[2] allows a recorded plea of guilty to one charge to be taken into consideration by the court if it involves an admission relevant to proof of another charge on the same complaint.

1 1961 JC 51.
2 1980 SLT (Notes) 53.

## The evidence of the accused

**2.09** No question of admissibility normally arises when the accused, in the course of giving evidence on oath, makes a confession or admission contrary to his interest. This will simply become part of the evidence against him. In *Ward v HM Advocate*[1] the accused was charged with murder. He had admitted assaulting the deceased to severe injury to the police and also at judicial examination and he repeated his admission on oath to the jury. Having been convicted of assault to severe injury he tried to withdraw the admission claiming that he had only made it for fear that he would be convicted of murder but the High Court held that it was too late to withdraw what had become in effect a judicial admission of guilt. In *Backhurst v MacNaughton*[2] it was held in unusual circumstances that an accused who had been tried on a charge of reset in the course of which he had admitted the theft of certain of the articles in question could not be convicted of resetting these articles.

1 1993 GWD 9–590.
2 1981 SCCR 6.

## Admission of facts and documents

**2.10** Sections 150 and 354 of the 1975 Act allow facts and documents to be admitted in both solemn and summary procedure by lodging a written minute with the clerk of court, although the accused must be legally represented. A verbal admission is insufficient.[1] Apart from statutory authority, no fact can be established in a criminal trial by admissions on the part of the accused since a person accused of crime is not in a position to make admissions with safety to himself.

Admissions made without statutory authority by the accused's agent are likewise incompetent.[2]

1 *Jessop v Kerr* 1989 SCCR 417.
2 *Tullis v Millar* (1899) 3 Adam 3.

## Judicial examination

*Historical aspects*

**2.11** The detailed rules which governed the old form of judicial examination or judicial declaration are now really only of historical interest. However, the existence of the declaration procedure coloured the attitude of the Scottish courts towards police questioning until the 1960s and accordingly a brief outline will be given here.[1]

1 For a fuller treatment reference may be made to Alison *Practice*, Chap XIII; Dickson *The Law of Evidence in Scotland* §§ 327–336; and G H Gordon 'The Institution of Criminal Proceedings in Scotland' (1968) 19 NILQ 249.

**2.12** In broad terms, a prisoner who had been apprehended would be brought before a magistrate, normally though not invariably the sheriff, in order to 'emit a declaration'. Although this phrase suggests the spontaneous making of a voluntary statement, the prisoner would generally be interrogated. In theory the questioning was carried out by the magistrate but in practice, and despite judicial disapproval, much of it was done by the procurator fiscal. The prisoner was not placed on oath but he had to be 'judicially admonished' that he was not bound to answer any questions but that if he did answer what he said would be written down and might be used in evidence against him at his trial.

**2.13** The taking of a declaration was frequently a lengthy process and might be repeated if more evidence became available. There appears to have been a considerable degree of procedural flexibility. For instance William Roughead must bring a tear to the eye of many a modern prosecutor when he recounts a known instance of the prisoner being taken to the scene of the crime, being questioned there and being shown a dead body and asked questions about it.[1]

1 'The Dunecht Mystery' in *Twelve Scots Trials* p 259.

**2.14** If the declaration was proved to have been freely and voluntarily emitted by the accused it was admissible against him at his subsequent trial. Provided the declaration itself was admissible, any confession or admission which it contained would thus become part of the evidence against the accused at his trial. A declaration might be ruled inadmissible for various reasons including excessive interrogation, inducement, the drunkenness or insanity of the prisoner at the time of emitting it or the fact that the prisoner had previously been precognosced on oath as a witness.

**2.15** No clear rule emerged on the admissibility of a declaration emitted on a charge different from that on the indictment, although it would appear from *James Stewart*[1] and *Macdougall v MacLullich*[2] that the declaration would be admissible where the indictment was a *lesser* charge arising from the same *species facti* but not where it was more serious.

1 (1866) 5 Irv 31.
2 (1887) 14 R(J) 17.

**2.16** The judicial declaration declined in importance following the case of *HM Advocate v Brims*[1] and more particularly following the Criminal Evidence Act 1898 which for the first time gave an accused person the right to give evidence in his own defence.

1 (1887) 1 White 462.

*Criminal Justice (Scotland) Act 1980 procedures*

**2.17** The 1980 Act introduced a revised and rather toned down version of judicial examination to which reference has already been made.[1] If a judicial examination is held the transcript must be lodged as a production[2] and is admissible in evidence without being spoken to by witnesses.[3] Either prosecution or defence may apply to the court to refuse to allow a part or the whole of the transcript to be received.[4] The following have been suggested as possible grounds: disclosure of previous convictions; reference to other charges not on the indictment; reference to an extra-judicial confession which has been held inadmissible; irregularity in the conduct of the examination such as a departure from the statutory principles regarding questioning by the prosecutor.[5]

1 Para 1.17 above.
2 1975 Act, s 78(2); *HM Advocate v Cafferty* 1982 SCCR 444.
3 Ibid, ss 151(1) and 352(1).
4 Ibid, ss 151(2) and 352(2).
5 *Macphail* § 20.14C. *HM Advocate v Leitch* Glasgow High Court 1982, unreported.

**2.18** If the transcript or the appropriate part of it is admissible any statement or admission which it contains becomes part of the evidence against the accused. Sheriff Macphail puts it thus:

'If in the course of the examination the accused has made a material admission, as that he was present at the locus of the crime charged when it was committed, or that he was implicated in certain of the events comprised in the charge, or if he has made statements suggesting special knowledge of these events, such admissions or statements may provide corroboration of other evidence to the same effect, in the same way as other statements made by him either extrajudicially or in the witness box.'[1]

1 *Macphail* § 20.14D

**2.19** Although the High Court has sometimes hinted at some sort of special rules for statements at judicial examination,[1] these ideas have not been developed and it would appear that the normal rules relating to the admissibility of 'mixed' statements[2] apply to statements made at judicial examination. Thus, if in the course of judicial examination the accused makes an admission but qualifies it (for example admitting the blow but claiming self-defence) the position appears to be that where the statement is led by the Crown or by the defence without objection the whole statement is admissible as evidence of the facts it contains, the assessment thereof being a matter for the jury.

1 Eg *Morrison v HM Advocate* 1990 SCCR 235.
2 Para 3.10 ff below.

## Other judicial proceedings

### *Previous civil action etc*

**2.20** *Dickson*[1] states: 'As no person has a just reason to complain of his deliberate statements being used in evidence against him, those which a party has made in one cause may in general be used against him in another cause, although with a different opponent'. Although there is little modern authority, the accepted view is that in modern practice the evidence which he gave on oath in a previous civil action or judicial inquiry (eg a fatal accident inquiry) is admissible against the accused at his trial.[2] Statute may make specific provision for such evidence to be admissible or inadmissible in particular circumstances.[3]

1 Page 210, § 288.
2 Lewis *A Manual of the Law of Evidence in Scotland* p 318; Walker and Walker *The Law of Evidence in Scotland* p 31, § 33; *Renton and Brown* para 18–21; *Banaghan v HM Advocate* (1888) 1 White 566; *McGiveran v Auld* (1894) 1 Adam 448.
3 Eg Bankruptcy (Scotland) Act 1985, s 47(3)(a).

*Crown witness*

**2.21** It is sometimes thought that a witness who gives evidence for the Crown at a criminal trial thereby becomes immune from prosecution in respect of an offence emanating from the same incident, but this view is incorrect. In reality immunity only extends to a *socius criminus* and then only in respect of the libel in support of which he has given evidence.[1] It therefore follows that if a Crown witness makes a self-incriminatory statement that may become admissible against him if he is subsequently prosecuted.

1 *O'Neill v Wilson* 1983 SCCR 265 approving *McGinley & Dowds v MacLeod* 1963 JC 11; cf *Jones and Collins v HM Advocate* 1991 SCCR 290.

*Defence witness*

**2.22** A witness for the defence in a criminal trial knows no immunity from prosecution and anything which he says in evidence may be admitted against him subsequently. It is routine for such a witness to be warned that he need not incriminate himself. Although there does not appear to be any authority on whether the absence of a warning would render the statement inadmissible against its maker, it would appear to offend against the principle of fairness to admit a statement as evidence against its maker when he had been sworn 'to tell the truth, the whole truth and nothing but the truth' and possibly believed himself liable to punishment for prevarication if he failed to answer questions.

# EXTRA-JUDICIAL CONFESSIONS – THE POLICE

## History

**2.23** The rise of the modern police was essentially a phenomenon of the nineteenth century, although 'constables' appointed by the Justices of the Peace had been in existence in Scotland since the early part of the seventeenth century and in addition many towns employed watchmen.[1] A constable was required to take anyone he arrested to a magistrate forthwith so that the person could be dealt with according to law. There was no clear transition to the modern form of policing which took place at different times in different areas. Aberdeen obtained the first private police Act in Scotland in 1795 and Glasgow followed suit in 1800. The latter city appointed its first 'criminal officer' (ie detective) in 1819. Legislation in the middle of the nineteenth century facilitated, and latterly required, local authorities to establish police forces and by the end of the century Scotland was fully policed in the modern sense.

1 See generally Hume *Commentaries* II 76; J Irvine Smith *Introduction to Scottish Legal History* (Stair Society vol 20) p 40 and pp 427–428.

**2.24**   The modern form of policing was unknown to Hume and when he talks of the 'criminal police' it would appear that he was referring to officials connected with the administration of justice. Thus it is necessary to turn to Burnett, writing in 1811, for the earliest observations on confessions to police officers. Like Hume, Burnett considered that extra-judicial verbal confessions made at the time of detection, accompanied with entreaties of forgiveness, and sorrow for what had happened, and addressed, 'not to the inferior officers of justice, whose severity he may dread, and wish by any means to deprecate', but to the parties injured, were strong and important circumstances, though not of themselves conclusive. Burnett considered that the value of such confessions was diminished if they had been obtained by 'undue means' and they were wholly inadmissible if obtained by threats or promises. His conclusion was unflattering to the contemporary police:

'Hence it is that from the influence which the inferior officers of police are supposed to have over those whom they are employed to apprehend, as well as from the bias, and even interest which their situation creates, to lead them to misrepresent or misapprehend words uttered by the accused, their evidence on this subject ought always to be received with caution and distrust.'[1]

1 Page 530.

**2.25**   *Alison* had little to say on the subject of confessions to the police. By the time of Dickson a body of case law was beginning to build up and although Dickson was much less hostile to the police than Burnett, he was, as will be discussed later, still wary of them, particularly the danger of fabricated confessions.[1]

1 *Dickson* § 378. See further paras 5.35–5.36 below.

*A look at the nineteenth-century cases*

**2.26**   The Scottish courts began to address the issue of confessions to the police against the background of the judicial declaration and the low status enjoyed by the early police. As there was no appeal from a decision of the High Court until 1926, the early cases on confessions to the police are mostly single-judge decisions taken at first instance and are occasionally inconsistent. At first the courts tended to deal with evidence resulting from police questioning (as opposed to spontaneous utterances which, as already noted, have always been admissible) on the basis of competency, although the first reference to the issue being one of fairness came in Lord Young's judgment in *Gracie v Stuart*.[1] Certain general principles became established at a fairly early stage although a very wide judicial discretion existed. It was also by no means uncommon for a judge to express disapproval of police conduct but at the same time admit the evidence.

1 (1884) 5 Coup 379.

**2.27**   The very first reported case on the admissibility of a confession to the Scottish police was *Robert Alexander and John McCourt*[1] where a criminal officer gave evidence that while escorting McCourt through the streets he questioned him about the charge against him and McCourt confessed, implicating Alexander. He said he had said nothing to induce the confession and the evidence was admitted despite 'some doubt' being entertained on the bench as to its regularity.

1 (1831) Bell's Notes 244.

**2.28**   Although evidence obtained by questioning at or around the time of apprehension was generally admitted,[1] one trend which quickly emerged was the judicial dislike of inquisitorial questioning in the police station. Although the first case on this point, *Lowrie and Cairns*,[2] was actually in favour of admitting the evidence the courts' attitude quickly hardened, and following *John Martin and Catherine Robb*[3] evidence arising from questioning after lodging in the police office was generally considered inadmissible.[4]

1 *Agnes Christie or Paterson* (1842) 1 Broun 388; *Lewis v Blair* (1858) 3 Irv 16; *William Wylie* (1858) 3 Irv 218; *Isabella Laing* (1871) 2 Coup 23; *Gracie v Stuart* (1884) 5 Coup 379.
2 (1836) Bell's Notes 244.
3 (1842) 1 Broun 382.
4 *Dickson* p 242, § 347. See also *Theodore Dowd* (1852) J Shaw 575; *Isabella Laing* (1871) 2 Coup 23; *John Bruce aka Wood* (1842) Bell's Notes 245; *Catherine Beaton or Bethune* (1856) 2 Irv 457.

**2.29**   A related theme which recurs again and again was the High Court's dislike of police officers usurping the function of the magistrate at the judicial declaration and acting as 'examinators' of prisoners. This was first made express in *Catherine Symon*[1] where Lord Medwyn pointed out that by questioning the prisoner the police had done what the magistrate and no-one else was entitled to do, although he actually ruled in favour of admitting the evidence.

Subsequently, in *Helen Hay*[2] a criminal officer enquiring into a murder had apprehended the accused without a warrant on the basis of 'common report' that she had been guilty of the crime. He questioned her and she made replies which were presumably incriminating. At her trial objection was taken to evidence of this conversation on the basis that it amounted to a declaration taken without cautioning and without the protection of the magistrate. Crown counsel sought to argue that confessions and admissions made at the time of arrest without improper inducement had been repeatedly admitted in evidence but the objection was upheld by the Lord Justice-Clerk who pointed out to the police 'that when a person is under suspicion of a crime, it is not proper to put questions, and receive answers, except before a magistrate'.[3]

1 (1841) Bell's Notes 245.
2 (1858) 3 Irv 181.
3 See also *John Bruce aka Wood* (1842) Bell's Notes 245; *John Martin and Catherine Robb* (1842) 1 Broun 382; *Catherine Beaton or Bethune* (1856) 2 Irv 457. Cf *John Thomson aka Peter Walker* (1857) 2 Irv 747 where despite adverse judicial comment the evidence appears to have been admitted without defence objection.

**2.30**  Professor A D Gibb has observed[1] that it says much for Scottish police methods that the books contain virtually no account of statements extracted by actual or threatened violence. However it was recognised early that any malpractice by the police such as pressure, inducement, deceit, even of a minor nature, or an attempt to entrap a prisoner into making a confession would result in the evidence of such confession or admission being excluded.[2] Even if the deceit had been for a good reason, for example to persuade a mentally-disturbed accused to 'come quietly', and not intended to entrap him into a confession, the evidence would still be held inadmissible.[3] In one extreme case it was held that evidence of a conversation between a female prisoner and a policeman's wife was inadmissible even though it was clear that there had been no improper motive. The mere possibility of the accused being entrapped into a confession was sufficient to exclude the evidence.[4]

1 (1954) 66 JR 199 at 207.
2 *Dickson* p 240, § 344. *Ann Watt or Ketchen* (1834) Bell's Notes 244; *Kerr v Mackay* (1853) 1 Irv 213; *Ditrich Mahler and Marcus Berrenhard* (1857) 2 Irv 634.
3 *George Bryce* (1864) 4 Irv 506.
4 *May Grant* (1862) 4 Irv 183; cf *John Millar* (1859) 3 Irv 406.

**2.31**  Provided there had been no attempt to entrap, any confessions or admissions volunteered or blurted out to the police were admissible even though no caution had been given. The clearest statement of this was in *Smith v Lamb*.[1] The accused, on the day he had been liberated on bail, approached the policeman who had arrested him and engaged him in conversation in the course of which certain admissions were made and which were used in evidence at his trial. The High Court had no trouble in dismissing the appeal, Lord McLaren observing that:

'The appellant went up to the constable and spoke about his case. It is no part of the duty of a police constable to warn every person who casually addresses him not to say anything in case it may be used in evidence against him.'

1 (1888) 15 R(J) 54.

**2.32** Although a wide judicial discretion was used, by the end of the nineteenth century the law had generally reached the following position. The prime duty of the police officer was to apprehend an offender and bring him before the magistrate for examination. It was no part of his duty to interrogate the prisoner or attempt to obtain a confession of guilt and the questioning of a prisoner in custody, if not actually prohibited, was strongly discouraged. However, evidence of a statement made by a prisoner to a police officer would be admissible if: (i) it was made at or shortly after the time of arrest; (ii) it was made freely and voluntarily; (iii) it was made after he had been informed of the charge against him and preferably, though not necessarily, after he had been cautioned; (iv) there had been no more questioning than was absolutely necessary in the circumstances and the questioning had related to the subject matter of the charge, and had arisen naturally without any intention to entrap or obtain evidence unfairly; (v) it was made without inducement by threats, bribes or false representations.[1]

1 Anon 'Police Evidence' (1896) 12 SLR 203; H H Brown 'The Evidence of the Accused in Criminal Procedure' (1898) 5 SLT 182.

**2.33** The trends and judicial attitude which had developed during the nineteenth century continued substantially unchanged until the 1920s[1] although the courts did gradually begin to acknowledge the legitimacy of investigative police questioning, at least in the early stages of the inquiry, as can clearly be seen in *Costello v Macpherson*.[2]

1 Eg *Hodgson v Macpherson* (1913) 7 Adam 118.
2 1922 JC 9.

**2.34** Nevertheless, *Waddell v Kinnaird*,[1] one of the few cases of the period where there is anything approaching a consideration of precedent, showed a remarkable lack of judicial unanimity in the High Court. The police had cautioned and charged a railway employee with theft but he was then questioned by a superior in the presence of the police without a further caution and certain statements were made which were admitted in evidence at the trial. On appeal the Lord Justice-Clerk and Lord Salvesen were both in favour of admitting the evidence but the former dealt with the question on the basis of competency, while the latter explicitly followed *Gracie v Stuart*[2] and considered that the matter was one of fairness. The third judge, Lord Ormidale, dissented vigorously and it was his judgment which was to have most influence on the subsequent development of the law. His Lordship, proceeding on the basis that although not carried out by them, the questioning had been at the instance of the police, drew a sharp distinction between a person who had not been charged with a crime and a person who had. In the former case the police were entitled in the due discharge of their duty to put questions before going on to arrest. However, once a person had been arrested the police had no right to put further questions, with or without caution, and such further questioning would mean that the police were constituting themselves 'examinators' of the prisoner. In Lord Ormidale's view:

'The insistence of an interrogation by the police of itself amounts to pressure and answers elicited under pressure are in an entirely different category from statements made spontaneously and of the prisoner's own accord'.

1  1922 JC 40.
2  (1884) 11 R(J) 22.

*The move towards an exclusionary rule*

**2.35**   Sheriff Gordon has described *Waddell v Kinnaird* as 'in a sense the last nineteenth-century case' and it clearly showed the two divergent possible approaches to evidence obtained by police questioning – on the one hand Lord Salvesen's approach which favoured judicial discretion based on fairness or some comparable test and on the other hand Lord Ormidale's approach which favoured a firm rule rendering *ipso facto* inadmissible evidence obtained by police questioning after a certain stage, for example arrest, had been reached. In fact, although it was to move a long way towards it between the 1920s and the 1950s, it can now been seen in retrospect that Scottish law never actually achieved a firm exclusionary rule in relation to police questioning, apart from the rule that a statement obtained by questioning on a matter with which the accused has been charged is inadmissible.[1] At the same time as they were moving in the direction of an exclusionary rule, the courts began to adopt fairness to the accused as the basic test of the admissibility of confession evidence.

1  *Stark and Smith v HM Advocate* 1938 JC 170; *Wade v Robertson* 1948 JC 117.

**2.36** One issue with which the courts regularly had to deal at this period was the practice of the police detaining 'on suspicion' persons against whom there was insufficient evidence to justify a charge. Although condoned by the courts this practice was technically illegal and was to remain so until the passing of the 1980 Act. A person who was 'detained on suspicion' had all the disadvantages of a person who had been arrested without any of the safeguards and such a person could remain in the hands of the police for a considerable period of time. This issue troubled the High Court on several occasions. In *HM Advocate v Aitken*[1] Lord Anderson, the first judge to attempt to 'flesh out' the fairness test, considered that the correct test of admissibility was whether it was fair in the particular circumstances of the accused. This would involve the court considering the nature of the charge being investigated, the mental capacity of the prisoner at the time the statement was made and the circumstances in which the statement was made. His Lordship went on to make clear his view that the courts ought to be more jealous to safeguard the rights of someone who had been detained. His Lordship also made the pertinent point that if the evidence was weak the police might be tempted to buttress it by getting a statement from the prisoner and thus justifying the detention. Lord Anderson's view of the fairness test was approved by an appellate bench in *Mills v HM Advocate*.[2]

1  1926 JC 83.
2  1935 JC 77.

**2.37** Passing reference has been made to the case of *Stark and Smith v HM Advocate*[1] which led to the only true exclusionary rule to affect confession evidence in Scotland. In *Stark* the actions of both the police and the trial court were really quite extraordinary. The two accused had been committed for further examination in custody on a charge of theft. Notwithstanding the fact that he was under the protection of the court, police officers visited Smith in custody and questioned him further about the offence which produced certain admissions. Not content with this they then brought him into Stark's presence and told the latter what his co-accused had said, Smith himself adding 'Yes I have told him everything'. Stark wisely refused to say anything. Unbelievable as it may seem today, at the trial Smith's statement was admitted as evidence against both accused. On appeal Lord Justice-General Normand laid down 'a salutary rule which ought to be observed in the future' that when a prisoner had been committed for further inquiry the police ought not to approach him on any question touching the crime with which he had been charged. It was the court's duty to see that the police did nothing which would prejudice his trial.

Some ten years later in *Wade v Robertson*[2] the High Court expanded the *ratio* of *Stark and Smith* and made it clear that once they have cautioned and charged someone with an offence the police are to all intents and purposes *functi* and any evidence obtained by subsequent questioning relating to that offence is inadmissible. The point was later re-emphasised in *HM Advocate v Davidson*.[3]

1  1938 JC 170.
2  1948 JC 117.
3  1968 SLT 17.

*The prelude to* Chalmers v HM Advocate

**2.38**  In *Bell v HM Advocate*[1] the then Lord Justice-General Cooper for the first time brought the strands of the earlier decisions together and laid down that a

'clear distinction must be drawn between admissions, confessions or other incriminating statements given or obtained from a person (1) who has been charged with a crime and is in custody awaiting trial, (2) who has been detained on suspicion, and (3) who has not been detained or charged, against whom there may be no evidence whatever justifying either detention or charge or even suspicion, but who is merely being questioned by the police in the exercise of their duties of investigating the commission of a crime.'

Although it was stated by Lord Mackay that 'the three quite separate sets of circumstances . . . give rise to equally different duties on the part of the police' the High Court was never to make express, either in *Bell* itself or in any subsequent case, exactly what the different duties were and later the view was taken that there were actually only two stages – before and after suspicion had focussed on the accused.[2] It was clear from *Bell* that any statement would be admissible, even in the absence of a caution, if it was made by an accused person to the police in the early stage of their enquiry when they did not suspect him to be the perpetrator, or when their suspicion was directed towards him only in the sense that he was one of a number of persons whose actions or movements required to be investigated.

1  1945 JC 61.
2  *Walker and Walker* p 38.

**2.39**  A short time later in *HM Advocate v Rigg*[1] Lord Cooper brought Scots law to what the fourth edition of *Renton and Brown* described as 'the high water mark of the anti-police approach to the question of unfairness'. Like a number of the other leading cases on confession evidence *Rigg* involved a youthful accused person charged with murder. Rigg was undoubtedly under suspicion when he made a statement to the police which, according to Lord Cooper meant that the police were under a special duty to observe every requirement of fairness which the law demands. It is difficult to see from the report exactly where the police were supposed to have failed this test since they appear to have treated Rigg humanely, cautioned him properly and offered him both parental presence and legal advice. Nevertheless Lord Cooper took the view that the statement could not have been made without questioning and thus could not be truly spontaneous and voluntary and he excluded it with the observation that:

'I am bound to say that I have viewed with growing uneasiness and distaste the frequency with which in recent years there have been tendered in support of prosecutions alleged voluntary statements said to have been made to the police by persons charged, then or subsequently, with grave crime.'

Professor A D Gibb,[2] in a splendidly colourful phrase, succinctly described the attitude of the High Court at this period as a 'feverish search for unfairness'.

1 1946 JC 1.
2 (1954) 66 JR 199 at 214.


*Chalmers v HM Advocate*

**2.40**   Eight years after *Rigg* Lord Cooper presided over the specially convened bench of five judges who sat to decide *Chalmers v HM Advocate*.[1] This case was a watershed and on the basis of the amount of attention it subsequently received both within and without Scotland it is one of the most famous cases ever decided by the High Court. No apology is offered for giving it detailed attention here.

1 1954 JC 66.


**2.41**   The facts of *Chalmers* are well known. The accused was a 16-year-old foundry worker who was charged with the robbery and murder of a fellow employee. Two days after the assault (and while the victim was still alive) he was interviewed by the police as part of their general inquiries and made his first statement dealing with his movements at the relevant time. About a fortnight later, the victim having meantime died, he was again interviewed by the police and made a second statement. About a week after that the police received information which tended to cast doubt on the two statements and decided to interview Chalmers again. The youth, who was now under suspicion, was brought to Falkirk police station having apparently been roused from bed sometime after ten am. He was cautioned and questioned by a detective inspector and after some questioning, which lasted only five minutes, but which the police admitted involved cross-examination, tears came into his eyes. The inspector cautioned him again and offered him the presence of his father or a solicitor, both of which Chalmers declined, saying he would make a statement. Another officer came into the proceedings to take this third statement and he again cautioned Chalmers and offered him the presence of his father or a solicitor, both of which were again declined. The statement was then taken down. Thereafter Chalmers was asked some more questions and, in consequence of the answers he gave, the police took him to a cornfield in Larbert where he showed them the whereabouts of the deceased's purse. Finally he was taken back to the police station where he was formally cautioned and charged in the presence of his father and made a fourth statement.

**2.42**  At the trial the first statement was led without objection, the second was not tendered by the Crown, the third was initially tendered but, objection having been taken, the Advocate Depute decided not to attempt to prove it. Nevertheless it was necessary for Lord Strachan, the trial judge, to consider the circumstances of its making to rule on the admissibility of the evidence of the visit to the cornfield and the fourth statement. The defence argued that evidence of the third statement would be inadmissible because the police proceedings by which it was obtained were unfair and the subsequent events, ie the visit to the cornfield and the reply to caution and charge, were tainted with the same unfairness.

**2.43**  In the view of the trial judge it was clear that at the material time Chalmers was a person 'detained on suspicion' and thus fell within the second category in *Bell v HM Advocate*.[1] Accordingly the interrogation to which he had been subjected was unfair and also contrary to the rule stated by *Dickson*[2] that the examination of the prisoner was not a police function. His Lordship pointed out that a caution was not a preliminary which would regularise cross-examination by the police. Although the circumstances of the taking of the third statement had been fair, it followed so closely on the unfair interrogation that the statement was tainted thereby. However, in the absence of authority, his Lordship decided to rule in favour of admitting the evidence of the visit to the cornfield and the recovery of the purse. He also took the view, with hesitation, that the reply to caution and charge (the fourth statement) was admissible due to the lapse of time since the interrogation and also since the police conduct had been fair at that stage. Chalmers was convicted and appealed.

1  1945 JC 61.
2  Page 242, § 347.

**2.44** Although it was not strictly before the appeal court, the admissibility of the third statement was obviously an important issue and the court permitted it to be argued. The Crown, somewhat forlornly, attempted to argue that since Chalmers had not been arrested the police could interrogate him provided there was no improper pressure. It also argued, under reference to *Lawrie v Muir*[1] which deals with the admissibility of evidence obtained by an irregular search, that even if there had been an irregularity it did not follow that the statement was inadmissible. Lord Cooper, while recognising that there was a distinction between routine exploratory questioning and interrogation after arrest, was in no doubt that the statement was inadmissible:

'But when a person is brought by police officers in a police van to a police station, and, while there alone, is faced with police officers of high rank, I cannot think that his need for protection is any less than it would have been if he had been formally apprehended. The ordinary person (least of all a youth of sixteen) is not to know that he could have refused to be taken to the police station or to answer any questions and, even if he knew that, he would be unlikely to adopt such a course and it would probably avail him little if he did.'

A statement obtained by the methods used in this case could not possibly be said to be 'voluntary' or 'spontaneous'.

1 1950 JC 19.

**2.45** The High Court overturned Lord Strachan on both the visit to the cornfield and the fourth statement. The question of 'confirmation by subsequent fact' will be considered later[1] and at this stage it is sufficient to note that Lord Cooper considered the accused's actings in the field to be indistinguishable from a statement as to the whereabouts of the purse which, in his Lordship's view, would have been inadmissible. Accordingly the evidence about the circumstances surrounding the finding of the purse (although apparently not the actual finding itself) was equally inadmissible. His Lordship also considered that the reply to caution and charge was inadmissible although he preferred to rest his final decision to quash the conviction on the ground that once the recovery of the purse was eliminated there was insufficient evidence.

1 Para 3.35 ff below.

**2.46** In a sense the facts in *Chalmers* are almost irrelevant since the main importance of the case lies in the views expressed by Lord Cooper and Lord Justice-Clerk Thomson on the general subject of police questioning and related procedures. Lord Cooper commented adversely on the practice of detention 'on suspicion'. Like Lord Anderson in *Aitken*[1] Lord Cooper pointed out that detaining a person on suspicion put him in much the same position as a suspect who had been arrested but deprived him of the privileges and safeguards to which an arrested person was entitled. According to Lord Cooper the police station was regarded by most people as a 'sinister' venue, and the dice were loaded against the suspect who was usually alone when confronted by several police officers, often of high rank, and who had no-one to corroborate him as to what took place.

1 1926 JC 83.

**2.47** Although he made the conventional noises of sympathy for the police in the 'difficult position in which they are often placed, Lord Cooper explicitly declined to lay down rules for their guidance, quoting a passage from Lord Sumner's speech in the Privy Council case of *Ibrahim v R*[1] to the effect that the decision to exclude evidence of statements by an accused was a matter of judicial discretion. However, Lord Cooper was at pains to point out that Scots and English law were not the same and the English courts would admit certain evidence which would be rejected in Scotland. It was not the function of the police when investigating a crime to direct their endeavours to obtaining a confession from the suspect. Any self-incriminating statement tendered before a Scottish court would be jealously examined, in light of all the proven circumstances, to ensure that it was spontaneous and if it did not satisfy that test evidence of the statement would usually be excluded. The ghost of the judicial declaration before a magistrate was also raised, somewhat inconclusively, and coupled with the curious suggestion that such a procedure might be used before arrest, although Lord Cooper later claimed that he was only restating the existing law.

1 [1914] AC 599 at 614.

**2.48** In a much quoted, and not infrequently misunderstood, passage his Lordship laid down that:

'The theory of our law is that at the stage of initial investigation the police may question anyone with a view to acquiring information which may lead to the detection of the criminal; but that, when the stage has been reached at which suspicion, or more than suspicion, has in their view centred upon some person as the likely perpetrator of the crime, further interrogation of that person becomes very dangerous, and if carried too far, eg to the point of extracting a confession by what amounts to cross-examination, the evidence of that confession will almost certainly be excluded.'

**2.49**   Lord Cooper explained the prohibition on police interrogation on the basis of the right to silence – an accused person could not be compelled to give evidence at his trial, and if the police were entitled to interrogate him and adduce evidence of what he said, that would have the effect of making the accused a compellable witness. It would also mean that the prosecution would be laying before the court at second hand evidence which could not be adduced at first hand.

**2.50**   The judgment of Lord Justice-Clerk Thomson is shorter and clearer than that of Lord Cooper, with whom he concurred. Lord Thomson acknowledged that in the course of routine police enquiries the person ultimately charged might be interviewed and, provided there was no bullying or other impropriety, the answers to ordinary and legitimate questions would be admissible. However, in another famous passage his Lordship went on:

'But there comes a point of time in ordinary police investigation when the law intervenes to render inadmissible as evidence answers even to questions which are not tainted by [improper] methods. After the point is reached, further interrogation is incompatible with the answers being regarded as a voluntary statement, and the law intervenes to safeguard the party questioned from possible self-incrimination.'

His Lordship appreciated that the crucial point was difficult to define but nevertheless considered that the honest and conscientious policeman ought to realise when the person he is questioning comes under serious consideration as the perpetrator of the crime. His Lordship continued:

'Once that stage of suspicion is reached, the suspect is in the position that thereafter the only evidence admissible against him is his own voluntary statement. A voluntary statement is one which is given freely, not in response to pressure and inducement, and not elicited by cross-examination. This does not mean that, if a person elects to give a statement, it becomes inadmissible because he is asked some questions to clear up his account of the matter, but such questions as he is asked must not go beyond elucidation. It is important to keep in mind also that the point of time when the axe falls is not necessarily related to the person being in custody or detention of some sort. The fact that he is detained may point to his being under suspicion but he may come under suspicion without being detained.'

**2.51**   *Chalmers* was clearly intended by the judges to settle the law on police interrogation for the future and, in the short term, as Sheriff Gordon has pointed out,[1] the case was taken by most Scottish lawyers and police officers to have established (1) that statements by a suspect in answer to police questioning were not admissible as evidence, at any rate if given in a police station; (2) that the police have no power to detain a suspect without charging him; and (3) that improper questioning could not be cured by cautioning. It was regarded as laying down a firm exclusionary rule and the only scope for manoeuvre lay in deciding when a person became a suspect. However, Sheriff Gordon also points out that on closer examination the decision does not necessarily support any such firm rule since Lord Cooper stressed the facts of the case, denied any power to give instructions to the police, and made frequent use of qualifying words and phrases.

1 Gordon *Admissibility* p 330.

**2.52** From the perspective of 40 years later, it can now be seen that the influence of *Chalmers* on the development of the law of evidence was more apparent than real. For one thing Lord Cooper retired shortly after *Chalmers* and died the following year. His successor, Lord Justice-General Clyde, was obviously of a different mind and indeed one may wonder what would have happened in cases such as *Manuel v HM Advocate*[1] if Lord Cooper had still been presiding over the appeal court. The police themselves do not appear to have regarded *Chalmers* as bringing about any change in the interpretation of the law.[2] There were comparatively few reported cases on police questioning during the rest of the 1950s and by the mid-1960s the retreat from *Chalmers* was well established. Indeed, the next important case in which confession evidence played a major part, *Manuel*, shows a perceptible relaxation of judicial attitude a mere four years after *Chalmers*. Never again was the High Court to take such a strict line on police questioning.

1 1958 JC 41.
2 See [1961] Crim LR 70.

**2.53** The most lasting influence of *Chalmers* has probably been in procedural matters, since Lords Cooper and Thomson laid down that where there was a dispute over the admissibility of a statement to the police the judge should hear the evidence outwith the presence of the jury. If he ruled in favour of admitting it the evidence would be led a second time before the jury. If he ruled against, the jury would hear nothing of the matter. Thus the trial-within-a-trial, similar to the English *voire dire* was introduced into Scottish procedure. This issue is discussed in more detail later.[1]

1 Chapter 4 below.

*The transition to the modern law*

**2.54** By the mid-1960s the attitude of extreme suspicion of the police which the High Court had shown in cases such as *Rigg*[1] and

*Chalmers* was waning and there was a growing acceptance that police questioning was a necessary part of the investigation of crime. The clearest indication of the impending departure from *Chalmers* came in *Brown v HM Advocate*[2] where the facts are uncannily similar to the earlier case. Once again the police were inquiring into a murder and theft and their suspicions had focussed on the accused. They informed him that there were discrepancies between his statement and other information which they wished to clarify. The accused had previously been cautioned and this was done again. However before any question was asked the accused broke down and said 'I kill't her'. He was then cautioned and charged with murder. Later he took the police to a park where the murder weapon was recovered and to a point near his home where the deceased's purse was found. The similarities with *Chalmers* are immediately apparent, right down to the tears, although the report does not say how old the accused was. However, after a trial-within-a-trial, the trial judge repelled an objection to the admission of the confession and the finding of the real evidence and Brown was convicted.

1  1946 JC 1.
2  1966 SLT 105.

**2.55**  At the hearing of Brown's appeal, the defence founded strongly on *Chalmers*, arguing that since the stage of suspicion had been reached, the police had no right to question him further and, moreover, to start to put other people's evidence to him was, in the circumstances, tantamount to cross-examination. If the confession was tainted, the subsequent finding of the knife and purse was likewise tainted. In refusing the appeal, the High Court, Lord Justice-General Clyde, Lord Migdale and Lord Cameron, began the process of reinterpreting *Chalmers* which would ultimately cause that case, in Sheriff Gordon's words, 'to disintegrate into yet another assertion that the only criterion is fairness'. All three judges stressed the absence in the present case of any undue pressure, bullying or inducement by the police. Lord Clyde accepted that the border between legitimate and tainted questioning was a difficult matter which would vary from case to case. Indeed his Lordship expressly warned against laying too much stress on the circumstances of individual cases and the resulting creation of subtle distinctions. In his Lordship's opinion:

'It is not possible to lay down *ab ante* the precise circumstances in which answers given to the police prior to a charge being made are admissible in evidence at the ultimate trial or where they are inadmissible. This is so much a question of the particular circumstances of each case and those circumstances vary infinitely from one another. But the test in all of them is the simple and intelligible test which has worked well in practice – has what has taken place been fair or not?'

**2.56** There are two main points of interest in *Brown*. Firstly, the court can be seen to adopt a narrow view of the term 'suspect' in the context of police questioning, restricting it in effect to the prime or only suspect. In the present case, although the police did, on their own admission, regard Brown as a suspect, they were still in the process of eliminating other people from the inquiry and thus, according to Lord Clyde, it was not in the least unfair of them to try to clear the matter up since they were still in the investigative stage. Secondly, Lord Cameron pointed out that while interrogation designed to lead to self-incrimination by a suspect goes far beyond the limit of permissible and legitimate inquiry,

'[I]t is also clear that not all answers to all questions addressed to a person under concentrated suspicion are necessarily inadmissible. The principle of fairness to an accused can and should always be invoked and applied to protect him from improper pressures or inducements or bullying in order to extract incriminating evidence or confessions of crime, but at the same time in obvious public interest it is undesirable to hamper unduly police officers legitimately engaged in the investigation and detection of crime.'

**2.57** Shortly afterwards Lord Cameron applied the reasoning of *Brown* in similar circumstances in *HM Advocate v McPhee*[1] where the police at the material time were starting to regard the accused as a 'mild' suspect although they thought that there was a chance that he might be a witness. The police inquiry was only at a preliminary stage and the field of suspicion had not narrowed itself down to one person, far less the accused.

1 1966 SLT (Notes) 83.

**2.58** The eclipse of *Chalmers* really began in the following year with the routine road traffic case of *Miln v Cullen*.[1] The circumstances of the case were straightforward. A collision had taken place between a lorry and a car and a short time later two policemen chanced on the scene. The lorry driver pointed Cullen out to the police as having been the driver of the car and opined that he was drunk. At this point Cullen was standing with a group of men about 100 yards from the scene of the accident. As the policemen went over to speak to him, he detached himself from the group whereupon one of the officers, Constable Blair, who had formed the opinion that he was unfit to drive, asked him if he was the driver of the car. No caution was given and the constable had no authority from the Chief Constable under section 232 of the Road Traffic Act 1960. Cullen admitted to having been the driver and he was then cautioned and charged.

1 1967 JC 21.

**2.59**   At the trial, the defence relied strongly on the earlier case of
*Foster v Farrell*[1] where, in similar circumstances, the Crown had conceded that the accused's admission of driving was inadmissible at
common law, a concession which was absent in *Miln v Cullen*. The
sheriff-substitute considered himself bound to follow *Foster* and disallowed the evidence of Cullen's admission with the result that he was
acquitted. The Crown having appealed, the High Court, Lord
Justice-Clerk Grant, Lord Strachan and Lord Wheatley, had no difficulty in holding that *Foster v Farrell* had no application in the present
circumstances since, as the result of the Crown's concession, it had
been concerned solely with the position under statute. In the circumstances of *Miln v Cullen* the only test to be applied was whether what
had taken place was fair or not. Lord Grant pointed out that 'incrimination' and 'unfairness' were far from being synonymous terms. The
court had to look at the realities of the situation. While the policemen
and the lorry driver had all formed the view that Cullen was unfit to
drive, the lorry driver's evidence that he had actually been driving was
uncorroborated. In that situation the constable, in asking the simple
question which he did, was not only acting reasonably, properly and
fairly but was acting in accordance with his duty. Although the Crown
conceded that Cullen was under suspicion at the material time, Lord
Grant was prepared to hold that matters had never progressed beyond
the stage of investigation. He also emphasised that fairness was not
unilateral:

'It is well to keep in mind that, in applying the test of fairness, one must not
look solely and in isolation at the situation of the suspect or accused: one must
also have regard to the public interest in the ascertainment of the truth and in
the detection and suppression of crime.'

1  1963 SLT 182.

**2.60**   The point of greatest interest, however, is Lord Wheatley's
judgment. After reviewing the facts and distinguishing *Foster v
Farrell*, his Lordship went on to address what he regarded as 'certain
misconceptions' which had arisen in the interpretation of *Chalmers*.
He stressed that the basic and ultimate test at all stages of a police
investigation was fairness. However,

'While the law of Scotland has always very properly regarded fairness to an
accused person as being an integral part of the administration of justice,
fairness is not a unilateral consideration. Fairness to the public is also a legitimate consideration, and in so far as police officers in the exercise of their
duties are prosecuting and protecting the public interest, it is the function of
the court to seek to provide a proper balance to secure that the rights of individuals are properly preserved, while not hamstringing the police in their

investigation of crime with a series of academic vetoes which ignore the realities and practicalities of the situation and discount completely the public interest.'

Even after caution and charge questioning was not necessarily inadmissible. All that *Chalmers* had decided was that at that stage questions or actions which induced statements which were not voluntary or spontaneous were *liable to be ruled* inadmissible. Although the point was not actually before the court, the new realism was also applied firmly to the judicial declaration, which Lord Wheatley regarded as 'manifestly impractical' in the multitude of cases which the police had to handle.

**2.61** In the case of a 'suspect', provided a caution was properly given and understood, it was in Lord Wheatley's opinion unrealistic to proceed on the basis that questions which might elicit answers which might tend to incriminate the accused should automatically be disallowed. To adopt such a rule would be to so circumscribe police investigation that the public interest, the protection of the public, and the administration of justice might be completely ignored. In the particular circumstances of *Miln v Cullen* Lord Wheatley pointed out that Constable Blair's question was directed solely to discovering whether Cullen had been the driver of the car, not in itself a criminal offence, and nothing more. The position might have been different if Blair had, without cautioning, tried to elicit from Cullen an admission of culpability for the accident or an admission that he was drunk. The officers were still at the point of initial investigation and such suspicion as they had was tenuous, resting only on the unsupported evidence of an interested party. They had to elicit the facts and obviously their first duty was to identify the driver of the car. Even when they had done so they still had to make further inquiries to ascertain whether the driver had committed an offence. Cullen's counsel had argued that at the very least the police should have cautioned the accused but Lord Wheatley pointed out that if the lorry driver had been unable to identify Cullen, the argument put forward by defence counsel would have meant that the police would have had to caution every person they interviewed, a proposition which 'cannot stand the scrutiny of any test of bilateral fairness'.

**2.62** This was a very long way indeed from the judicial attitude of a mere 13 years before. However, Lord Wheatley was clearly no lone voice. His views were quoted with approval in *Bell v Hogg*[1] where Lord Cameron, who had already made his position clear in *Brown* and *McPhee*, added further *obiter* observations on the question of fairness towards persons under suspicion. The test was, 'whether there had been unfairness or improper pressure or inducement exercised or offered in eliciting these replies. This is not a matter of police interrogation; it by no means follows that a person who has come under suspicion may not be further questioned and his replies given in evidence. This I think is implicit in the giving of a caution, otherwise a caution in the normal terms would be pointless.'

This contrasts starkly with the view of Lord Cooper in *Chalmers* who considered that the fact that the police decided to caution someone was indicative of their view that he was a likely perpetrator of the crime.

1 1967 SLT 290.

**2.63** The extent to which *Chalmers* had fallen from grace was clearly shown in *Thompson v HM Advocate*,[1] a case with many similarities to *Aitken*,[2] where both Lord Wheatley and Lord Justice-General Clyde suggested that *Chalmers* might have to be reconsidered. In *Thompson* Lord Clyde went so far as to quote the opinion of Parke B in the old English case of *R v Baldry*: 'I confess that I cannot look at the decisions without some shame when I consider what objections have prevailed to prevent the reception of confessions in evidence . . . justice and common sense have, too frequently, been sacrificed at the shrine of mercy'.[3]

1 1968 JC 61.
2 1926 JC 83.
3 (1852) 2 Den CC 430 at 445.

### The modern fairness test

**2.64** *Miln v Cullen* has remained the definitive statement of the modern law for more than a quarter of a century. That case marked the final interment of the judicial declaration and made it clear that the Scottish courts would now accept questioning by the police as a legitimate part of the investigation of crime. Although *Chalmers* had not been overruled (and still has not been) the perception of that case had altered radically.

**2.65** The fourth edition of *Renton and Brown* published in 1972 put it thus:

'The courts will now look with sympathy on the need of the police to ask questions in detecting and bringing home guilt to offenders, and in cases of doubt the courts may be expected to admit statements made in response to questioning which does not smack of unfairness, whether because it is oppressive, or is of the nature of cross-examination, or involves threats, inducement or trickery. The mechanics of this change have been twofold. They have involved some redefinition of the stage of suspicion, and also a rejection of the notion that the existence of suspicion is in itself a paramount consideration. Recent cases adopt Lord Cooper's view of *Chalmers* and emphasise its tentative and pragmatic aspects.'[1]

1 Page 378.

**2.66** It may be remarked in passing that it is not beyond doubt whether the later interpretation of Lord Cooper's judgment is entirely in accordance with his Lordship's true feelings and intentions. His trenchant observations in *Rigg*[1] and indeed the decision in *Chalmers* itself, which has been described as 'a decision which on any realistic criterion it is difficult to support'[2] are, it is submitted, more consistent with a firm exclusionary rule than a mere reiteration of the fairness test. Since *Chalmers* was a full bench decision it could only be overturned by a larger bench and the restrictive interpretation of the term 'suspect' avoided the need to overturn or even reconsider it. *Chalmers* was effectively neutralised by being simultaneously 'explained' and sidestepped.

1 1946 JC 1.
2 J W R Gray '*Chalmers* and After' [1970] JR 1.

**2.67** Subsequent cases have produced no appreciable change in the *Miln v Cullen* view of the fairness test. As will be shown later,[1] by the 1970s the trial-within-a-trial was falling out of favour and the question of admissibility was tending to be viewed on the basis of whether the trial judge was justified in letting disputed statements go to the jury rather than on the basis of whether the statement was or was not actually unfairly obtained.

1 Para 4.04 ff below.

**2.68** In *Jones v Milne*[1] Lord Justice-General Emslie pointed out that it was not the law of Scotland that a suspect's answers to police questioning would never be admissible. His Lordship regarded *Miln v Cullen* as showing that,

'[T]he objection is to interrogation in the proper sense of that word and to answers which can be seen to have been extracted from the suspect. . . . The mere fact that a suspected person is asked a question or questions by a police officer before or after being cautioned is not in itself unfairness, and if answers are to be excluded they must be seen to have been extracted by unfair means which place cross-examination, pressure and deception in close company.'

This would appear to suggest that something more than simple cross-examination (if there is such a thing) was now required before a statement would be rendered inadmissible. His Lordship later repeated his comments in *Lord Advocate's Reference (No 1 of 1983).*[2]

1 1975 JC 16.
2 1984 SLT 337.

**2.69** Similar views were expressed in *Murphy v HM Advocate*[1] where *inter alia* the court considered (but did not decide) the question of the 'chargeable suspect' ie a person against whom the police have sufficient evidence to justify a charge but who has not actually been charged. This concept had been introduced by the then Professor Gordon[2] and concerned the possibility that the police might deliberately delay charging someone in order to obtain further evidence from him. The 'chargeable suspect', it was suggested, was in the same position as a person who has actually been charged and any statement obtained by questioning was inadmissible. Although theoretically sound, the concept of the 'chargeable suspect' has never been judicially approved. *Murphy* also makes it clear that even if unfairness can be established at one point, that does not necessarily taint everything that comes thereafter.[3] The issue of credibility was for the jury and not the judge and thus 'if two possible interpretations can properly be put on the situation, one of which falls into the category of fairness and the other into the category of unfairness the judge should leave the determination of that issue to the jury'.

1 1975 SLT (Notes) 17.
2 *Renton and Brown* (4th edn) p 374. See now 5th edn para 18–33.
3 See also *Kane v HM Advocate* unreported, CO Circular A30/79.

**2.70** In *Balloch v HM Advocate*[1] the accused had initially been interviewed (at some length) as witness but the police noticed discrepancies in his statement and began to suspect his involvement in the murder. He was questioned further without cautioning and it was only when he broke down and said 'I did it for Marion's sake' that he was cautioned. He thereafter made detailed confession. The evidence was admitted and on appeal Lord Wheatley clearly set out what might be called the 'no reasonable jury' test of admissibility:

'[A] Judge who has heard the evidence regarding the manner in which a challenged statement was made will normally be justified in withholding the evidence from the jury only if he is satisfied on the undisputed relevant evidence that no reasonable jury could hold that the statement had been voluntarily made and had not been extracted by unfair or improper means. Applying that test to the instant case, we are of the opinion that, to say the least, the question was so open that the trial Judge acted perfectly correctly in allowing the issue to go to the jury for their determination.'

1 1977 JC 23.

**2.71**   *Balloch* showed the extent to which the High Court had abandoned the old test of whether a confession had been voluntary and it was clear that some lawyers were becoming concerned by the extent to which *Balloch* and the decisions leading up to it had removed from the police the check of a firm exclusionary rule.[1] These concerns can hardly have been alleviated by the decision in *Hartley v HM Advocate*[2] which prompted one writer to observe:

'The elasticity of the concept of fairness is no doubt of immense value to the courts in this delicate task of balancing but it is questionable whether in *Hartley* it has not been overstretched and whether the police, looking at the decision and acting on it might not in the not too distant future be called again to heel.'[3]

1 Anon 'A Question of Fairness' 1977 SLT 177.
2 1979 SLT 26.
3 Anon 'Interrogation and the Test of Fairness' 1979 SLT 189.

**2.72**   Once again, *Hartley* involved a youth of 17 charged with murder, on this occasion the murder by drowning of a five-year-old boy in a burn in Cumbernauld. Hartley had been working in the area and he had made two inconsistent statements to the police. He agreed voluntarily to remain with the police while further inquires were made, although in fact two senior officers had instructed that he be detained. It is not entirely clear from the report what happened during the ensuing period, but he was apparently 'seen' and presumably spoken to by several police officers. Eventually, about 12 hours later, he was seen by a detective superintendent who considered him a suspect. This officer cautioned Hartley, went over his statement in detail, showed him a photograph of the deceased and asked him if he had seen the child, which Hartley initially denied. Eventually he asked 'Are you sure?' at which point Hartley became agitated, made a short, garbled, non-incriminatory statement, then paused and said 'It was me'. He was again cautioned and made a clear confession. At some point he broke down and while the detective superintendent tried to comfort him, Hartley said that he wanted to tell everything, but when told that he would have to make a statement to officers not connected with the inquiry, said he would only talk to one particular policeman. This officer, a detective sergeant, was eventually brought to the police station. He again cautioned Hartley who once more admitted the crime, saying that he took 'turns' and became violent. Hartley was subsequently cautioned and charged with murder.

**2.73**   At the trial the line of evidence was objected to and there were also allegations of police brutality but the trial judge admitted the evidence and his decision was upheld by the High Court. Defence counsel argued that there were five factors which, taken together, branded the confession as improperly obtained, viz (1) the age of the accused, (2) the fact (not apparently known to the police) that he had been to a special school, (3) the fact that he had been in custody for 12 hours, (4) the fact that he had not slept, and (5) the fact that he had neither legal nor parental advice. However, their Lordships had no doubt that the police actions had been fair throughout. Lord Avonside, in commenting on Lord Cooper's judgment in *Chalmers*, said:

'Firstly, police officers may question a suspect so long as they do not stray into the field of interrogation. Secondly and most importantly, cross-examination is just what it means. It consists in questioning an adverse witness in an effort to break down his evidence, to weaken or prejudice his evidence, or to elicit statements damaging to him and aiding the case of the cross-examiner.'

Lord Grieve found 'some similarities' with the circumstances of *Rigg* but distinguished it on the basis that the facts of the present case disclosed no evidence of the kind of interrogation which Lord Cooper found to be present in *Rigg*. His Lordship was clear that questions along the line of 'Are you sure?', which was the nearest the police had come to cross-examination, could 'seldom be said to have been extracted by unfair means'. It was not illegitimate to question a suspect. His Lordship considered that what was illegitimate was '. . . to use means to extract from a potential accused extra-judicial admissions which could not have been extracted from such a person in judicial proceedings against him, an accused person not being a compellable witness'.

**2.74** It is not entirely clear what Lord Grieve meant by this passage but he appears to be referring to the opinion of Lord Cooper in *Chalmers*.[1] While this point may have some logic in the context of a firm exclusionary rule, it is, it is submitted, unsound in the context of an acceptance of the legitimacy of police questioning of suspects. Since an accused person is not a compellable witness at his own trial, it follows that he cannot be questioned *at all* unless he voluntarily enters the witness box, in which case the prosecutor becomes, by statute, entitled to cross-examine him. It does not assist the understanding of an already difficult area of the law to propound a test which is factually and legally a *non-sequitur*.

1 Paras 2.48–2.49 above.

**2.75** Lord Dunpark also distinguished *Rigg* and *Chalmers*. In his opinion:

'The police are entitled to question suspects about parts of their previous statements which appear not to fit into the jigsaw puzzle which the police are endeavouring to construct, and a self-incriminating response to the question "Are you sure?" is not necessarily inadmissible as evidence against the suspect at his trial.'

Later his Lordship appeared to consider that cross-examination amounted to more than interrogation:

'Interrogation there certainly was, but no leading or repetitive questions or any unfair pressure which could reasonably be classified as cross-examination and thus render the answers inadmissible as evidence against the accused. Indeed this confession emerged, not in answer to a question, but as a correction of his immediately preceding statement. . . . It has all the hallmarks of a truly spontaneous confession, and, in my opinion, the five background factors founded on by counsel for the accused cannot convert this voluntary confession into one improperly obtained.'

**2.76**   The modern fairness test virtually defies analysis. The cases just mentioned show only one of the many problems: the courts' inconsistent use of language. What is really meant by 'interrogation' and 'cross-examination' and what is objectionable? The High Court generally has been reluctant to go beyond simple reiteration that fairness is the criterion for admissibility and 'unfairness can take many forms' although it is clear that there must have been some form of impropriety and the courts require to consider the whole surrounding circumstances before reaching a decision. Some judges have tried to elaborate. Thus in *Tonge v HM Advocate*[1] when Lord Cameron said:

'It is, of course, well established that police officers are entitled to question a suspect as to his possible complicity in a crime which they are investigating, and that his replies will be admissible in evidence if they have not been extracted or compelled by unfair or improper means including threats, intimidations, offers of inducements, or cross-examination designed or intended to extract incriminating replies, but it is equally well recognised that in the case of one on whom suspicion . . . has centred . . . it is proper practice that any further questioning should be preceded by a caution in common form.'

Perhaps the best explanation came from Lord Justice-General Emslie who explained that:

'Where . . . the word "interrogation" or the expression "cross-examination" are used in discussing unfair tactics on the part of the police, they are to be understood to refer only to improper forms of questioning tainted with an element of bullying or pressure designed to break the will of the suspect or to force from him a confession against his will.'[2]

1  1982 SCCR 313, 1982 SLT 506.
2  *Lord Advocate's Reference (No 1 of 1983)* 1984 JC 52, 1984 SCCR 62.

**2.77** It may also be remarked that while there are undoubted reasons of policy for doing so, the modern practice of leaving the issue of fairness to the jury also militates against analysis of the law. If the rationale of the law is, as the Thomson Committee believed, the control of the police, it is on one view appropriate that the jury, representing the public, should determine what is acceptable. On the other hand the inscrutable verdict of a jury is hardly the best vehicle for sending messages to the police who could simply dismiss the verdict as being 'anti police' something which would be much more difficult if the reason for rejection of the evidence was spelled out by the judge.

## The fairness test in practice

### General

**2.78** It has long been the law that truly voluntary statements, as opposed to statements obtained by questioning, are admissible. There have been few modern cases dealing with the question of an incriminating statement blurted out or volunteered to a police officer and not obtained by questioning, but provided the police have done nothing to induce it, and the circumstances are otherwise fair such a statement is admissible.[1]

1 *Dickson* p 243, § 348; *Smith v Lamb* (1888) 15 R(J) 54; *Thomson v HM Advocate* 1968 JC 61.

### Preliminary stage

**2.79** The law on questioning at the preliminary stage has remained settled, at least since *Costello v Macpherson*.[1] Nobody has any obligation at common law to assist the police although in certain circumstances a refusal (or inability) to explain, for example, the source of stolen property, may be admissible as evidence against the accused.[2] On the other hand, in carrying out their preliminary inquiries into a crime, including whether a crime has actually been committed, the police are entitled to question anybody they wish without administering a caution.[3] Any statement made at this stage by a person subsequently tried for the offence will normally be admissible. In *Wingate v Mackinnon*[4] a case under section 1 of the Prevention of Crime Act 1953, the accused was asked, without cautioning, why he was carrying a pick axe handle and made an incriminating reply. On appeal it was held that there had been nothing unfair and it was pointed out that:

'Bearing in mind that the offence in this instance is having an offensive weapon without lawful authority or reasonable excuse, it can readily be understood that, if a preliminary question such as was put in the present case namely, why was he carrying the pick axe handle, had been preceded by a caution, the result might be to inhibit the person questioned from putting forward a reasonable excuse which he might have for having the weapon there. That reinforces our opinion that there was nothing objectionable in the asking of the question in this case although no caution had been administered.'

*Wingate v Mackinnon* reinforces the conclusion which had been reached in the earlier case of *Custerson v Westwater*[5] in which the defence had conceded that it was unobjectionable for the police to ask someone, who had been alleged to be in possession of a knife, whether he in fact had a knife. The question, which had been asked without caution, had resulted in the production of the knife and an incriminatory reply.

1 1922 JC 9.
2 Eg *Cryans v Nixon* 1955 JC 1; *Fox v Patterson* 1948 JC 104.
3 *Costello* above; *Bell v HM Advocate* 1945 JC 61.
4 High Court, 13 June 1989, unreported, CO Circular A27/89.
5 1987 SCCR 389.

*The stage of suspicion*

**2.80**  One of the main changes to result from the deliberations of the Thomson Committee was the enactment of section 2 of the Criminal Justice (Scotland) Act 1980 which gives the police a specific statutory power of detention for questioning for a maximum period of six hours. At the conclusion of the period the suspect must be arrested or released and cannot be further detained on the same grounds. This has ended the anomalous and largely unregulated practice of 'detention on suspicion' which was so severely criticised in *Chalmers* and other cases. Section 2 now puts it beyond doubt that (a) the police are entitled to question a person who is a suspect and (b) within the statutory framework they are entitled to detain him in custody for this purpose. Virtually identical powers have been given to officers of Customs and Excise by section 48 of the Criminal Justice (Scotland) Act 1987.

**2.81**  Section 2(5) expressly safeguards the existing common law rules of admissibility[1] and there is a curious provision in section 2(7) which requires the police to inform the accused both on detention and on arrival at the police station that he is under no obligation to answer any question other than to give his name and address. Any idea that this provision provided a substitute for a common law caution was soon quashed[2] and the High Court has now come to the view that section 2(7) imposes a purely procedural requirement to inform the accused of his duty to give his name and address, and when the accused has been properly cautioned omission of a section 2(7) warning at the time of detention is of no significance in relation to admissibility.[3]

1 See *HM Advocate v Mair* 1982 SLT (Notes) 471 and *Tonge v HM Advocate* 1982 SCCR 313.
2 *Tonge v HM Advocate* above.
3 *Scott v Howie* 1993 SCCR 81.

**2.82** Section 2 has simplified the question of when a person becomes a suspect. Clearly if he is detained under section 2 he is *ipso facto* under suspicion and the common law requires that he is given a full caution before being questioned – as already noted the limited warning provided for in section 2(7) is insufficient on its own. There have been few cases where the police have been caught deliberately trying to evade the provisions of section 2. In *HM Advocate v Caithness and Fraser*[1] Lord Ross held unfair evidence of an interview with a suspect when the police had arrested him at the conclusion of the six-hour detention period but had delayed charging him until they had questioned him further. In *Grant v HM Advocate*[2] the accused had been properly detained and questioned and had made an incriminating reply. However, he was not arrested until some twenty minutes after the six-hour period had expired. The High Court rejected an argument that this invalidated all that had gone before. It can probably be concluded that as long as any questioning takes place during valid detention and satisfies the requirements of the common law, any incriminatory statement elicited will be admissible even if there is some technical failure to comply with the letter of the section.

1 Dundee High Court 1985, unreported.
2 1989 SCCR 618.

**2.83** Apart from section 2 there continues the possibility of 'voluntary' attendance, whereby a person, almost certainly under some degree of suspicion, is invited to accompany the police to the police station and, on arrival, will be asked to sign a form stating that his attendance is voluntary and he agrees to remain with the police for interview. Presumably there is also no reason why somebody who has been detained and released from detention should not remain voluntarily with the police thereafter. Although there has, as yet, been no judicial consideration of the issue of 'voluntary' attendance, the common law will continue to be relevant and if the 'volunteer' is under suspicion, or suspicion focusses on him in the course of police questioning, he will require to be cautioned. Any failure to do so will, at the very least, put the admissibility of any statement at risk.[1] The same will apply where suspicion focusses on somebody who is neither a detainee nor a volunteer.

1 *Tonge v HM Advocate* 1982 SCCR 313.

**2.84** If a person in the hands of the police but not a suspect suddenly blurts out an incriminating statement before the police have the chance to caution him, that statement will be admissible.[1] On the other hand if the questioning (or other behaviour) is clearly unfair, no amount of cautioning will render the evidence admissible: 'Giving a caution does not justify an interrogator in conducting a searching and forceful cross-examination of a suspected person'.[2] The issue of cautioning is considered further later in this work.[3]

1 *Thomson v HM Advocate* 1968 JC 61.
2 *HM Advocate v Friel* 1978 SLT (Notes) 21 at 22; see also *HM Advocate v Mair* 1982 SLT (Notes) 471.
3 Para 2.93 below.

## Caution and charge

**2.85** Once the police have reached the stage of actually charging someone with an offence they will invariably caution him before reading over the charge. Any reply made will be admissible.[1] There is little case law on the question, but the practice of admitting such a reply is of such universal practice and long standing, having been described in the first edition of *Renton and Brown* in 1909, that it is beyond challenge. A full caution before a charge is made is now a requirement of the law itself.[2] A failure to caution, however unlikely, will accordingly result in a reply to a charge being held to be inadmissible. There is no rule of law that the accused must be afforded an opportunity to consult his solicitor before he is cautioned and charged.[3] A reply to caution and charge is admissible even though the police had insufficient evidence to justify the charge.[4]

1 *Walker and Walker* pp 39–40; Mill *The Scottish Police: Their Powers and Duties* p 89.
2 *Tonge v HM Advocate* 1982 SCCR 313 at 344 and 350; *Walker and Walker* p 40.
3 *Law v McNicol* 1965 JC 32.
4 *Heywood v Smith* 1989 SCCR 391.

**2.86** In one unusual case, *Johnston (D) v HM Advocate*,[1] the High Court held that replies to police questioning by a person who had been arrested and cautioned but not charged were admissible. It would thus appear that anything said by the accused to the police up to and including his reply to caution and charge is *prima facie* admissible and it is only after he has been charged (and has made any reply to the charge that he wishes) that a statement elicited by police questioning becomes inadmissible.[2]

1 1993 SCCR 693.
2 For further discussion see D B Griffiths 'Interviews with Suspects – Two Unusual Cases' Greens Criminal Law Bulletin, August 1993.

**2.87** There is a limited amount of older authority to the effect that a reply to caution and charge will be admissible even if it shows the accused to be of bad character[1] but any prosecutor seeking to adduce such a reply under modern conditions would be treading on thin ice and the disclosure of actual previous convictions would be liable to vitiate the entire prosecution.[2]

1 *HM Advocate v McFadyen* 1926 JC 93; *Renton and Brown* para 18–37, note 1a.
2 Cf *Graham v HM Advocate* 1983 SCCR 314.

*The stage following charge*

**2.88** Once a person has been cautioned and charged, a statement by him will be admitted only if it is truly voluntary, and the law is jealous to safeguard the accused's interests. It is not the law that after charge the police may have no further contact with the accused, indeed there may well be a legitimate reason for interviewing him further, such as the recovery of stolen property or the identification of accomplices, and any evidence thus discovered is probably admissible *quantum valeat*. It is, of course, possible that in this situation the accused might make incriminatory remarks 'off his own bat'. Although there is no reported decision dealing squarely with the point, it is thought that if the police are legitimately interviewing the accused for such a purpose and the court is satisfied that their questions were not designed to obtain additional incriminatory material from him, any incriminatory statement which the accused voluntarily chooses to make will be admissible against him. However, a statement obtained by questioning about the matter in relation to which the accused has been charged is almost certainly inadmissible.[1]

1 *Stark and Smith v HM Advocate* 1938 JC 170; *Wade v Robertson* 1948 JC 117; *HM Advocate v Davidson* 1968 SLT 17; cf *Fraser and Freer v HM Advocate* 1989 SCCR 82.

**2.89** If the police question the accused about *another* matter, ie a matter separate from the subject of the charge, any statement made in relation to the other matter will normally be admissible provided the second matter is not merely an enlargement or extension of the first.[1]

1 *Macdonald v HM Advocate* 1987 SCCR 581; *Carmichael v Boyd* 1993 SCCR 751.

**2.90**  It is, of course, wholly illegitimate for the police to induce the accused to make a statement or put any pressure on him to do so, for example by telling him he will be released from custody if he gives a statement. The court will require to consider all the circumstances but a simple answer by the police to a question asked by the accused is unlikely to result in a finding that the statement had been induced. Thus, in *Aiton v HM Advocate*[1] the accused had been cautioned and charged and was being taken to court when he asked the police if his co-accused was 'sticking him in'. The police cautioned him and then told him that the co-accused had made a statement although they gave no details. The accused then made an incriminating remark which was held to be admissible. Similarly in *Young v Friel*[2] it was held not to amount to inducement when the accused asked 'What will happen if I tell you? Will I get kept in?' and a police officer replied 'I can't offer you any deals at present'.

1  1987 SCCR 252.
2  1992 SCCR 567.

**2.91**  If the accused makes the statement for some reason of his own, for example because he believes it may assist a member of his family, that will not affect the issue of fairness provided that the police have done nothing to induce the belief.[1]

1  Eg *Manuel v HM Advocate* 1958 JC 41.

*Voluntary statement*

**2.92**  If the accused indicates a wish to make a voluntary statement, he should be offered the services of a solicitor.[1] It is unclear whether failure to offer the accused legal assistance will render the statement unfairly obtained[2] but any pressure to dispense with legal advice which has been requested, for example by an implied threat that the accused might spend longer in custody if he waited for the solicitor to arrive, is likely to result in the statement being held to have been unfairly obtained.[3] The accused should be cautioned before making the statement, even if he has been cautioned at an earlier stage. In *Tonge v HM Advocate*[4] the High Court said that 'the regular and proper practice' is for the statement to be taken by officers unconnected with the particular investigation. However, this is not a rule of law and it is not necessarily unfair for an officer involved in the inquiry to take the statement, at least not when the accused expressly requests to speak to him.[5] The fact that the statement was not taken by independent officers is simply an aspect of fairness for the jury to consider. The statement will normally be written by the police at the accused's dictation (although there is no reason why the accused should not write his own voluntary statement if he so wishes) and will be signed by the accused and the officers. Under modern conditions it may also be tape-recorded. Questioning should be kept to an absolute minimum and restricted to clearing up ambiguities.

1 *HM Advocate v Cunningham* 1939 JC 61.
2 See *Renton and Brown* para 18–37.
3 *Law v McNicol* 1965 JC 32.
4 1982 SCCR 313 at 350.
5 *Cordiner v HM Advocate* 1991 SCCR 652 at 665; cf *Rodgers v Hamilton* 1993 GWD 30–1863.

## The fairness test – some particular issues

*The fairness test and the caution*

**2.93**    The position of the caution in relation to the fairness test has changed somewhat over the years. It has already been noted[1] that a caution at the time of reading over a charge is now a requirement of the law. Apart from the stage of charging, in Scottish practice the fact that a caution had or had not been given was, until comparatively recently, regarded simply as one of the factors to be taken into account in assessing whether what had taken place between the police and the suspect was fair and the statement had been 'spontaneous and voluntary'. It scarcely needs to be said that if the police questioning is otherwise unfair no amount of cautioning will make the results admissible as was held in *HM Advocate v Friel*.[2] However, it is now clear that the caution itself has acquired something of a special status and, although it may be going too far to say that a caution is an essential prerequisite of the admissibility of a statement by a suspect, failure to caution in the proper terms at anything other than the preliminary stage of an inquiry will certainly put the admissibility of any incriminating statement at risk.

1 Para 2.85 above.
2 1978 SLT (Notes) 21.

**2.94**    The conventional wording of the modern common law caution is 'You are not obliged to answer but if you do, your answers will be noted and may be used in evidence'. Appropriate prefixes are added depending on the stage of the proceedings at which it is being given and if the interview is being tape-recorded this will be mentioned. Any police officer who departs from this formula does so at his peril as was demonstrated in *HM Advocate v Docherty*[1] where a police officer of high rank and long experience 'cautioned' a suspect '. . . I am going to ask you some questions. I must warn you that any answers you give will be noted and may be given in evidence'. What he did not tell the suspect was that he was not obliged to answer. Lord Cowie rejected the resulting statement pointing out that 'It is a basic right of every accused person (sic) to be allowed to remain silent when he comes under suspicion of a crime. . . . So there we have a case of an accused person under suspicion who is not informed of one of his basic rights'.

1 1981 JC 6.

**2.95**　The current (fifth) edition of *Renton and Brown* identifies the case of *HM Advocate v Von*[1] as the starting point for the trend towards giving the caution a special status. This was a decision by Lord Ross sitting as trial judge and not a decision by the appeal court. Von had been detained on a Saturday under the Prevention of Terrorism (Temporary Provisions) Act 1976, section 11 of which, broadly, penalises a person who has information about acts of terrorism and fails 'without reasonable excuse' to disclose that information to the police. The provisions of section 11 were drawn to his attention by the police but they omitted to mention the 'reasonable excuse' proviso. Von was interviewed several times and on the Sunday he informed the police he would make a statement regarding his own involvement but would not incriminate anyone else. At this point the police warned him that what he said could be used in evidence but did not administer a full caution. Lord Ross held the statement inadmissible on the basis that the accused had not been given sufficient warning that he was not obliged to incriminate himself.

1 1979 SLT (Notes) 62. See further para 2.106 below.

**2.96**　Reference has already been made[1] to the subsequent case of *Tonge v HM Advocate*[2] where the issue was rather confused by the then novel provisions of section 2 of the 1980 Act. In this case two youths, Tonge and Gray, were detained under section 2 on suspicion of rape. The evidence against them was, at best, thin and the temptation for the police to bolster it by obtaining incriminating statements must have been substantial. Gray was apparently cautioned at common law when he was detained and both were given the statutory warning under section 2(7) but neither was cautioned at common law before being interviewed. 'Interviewed' indeed may not be the correct description since what happened was that the police, without any preliminaries, simply accused the two of having participated in the crime. Both then proceeded to make incriminating statements. Objection was taken to the statements at the trial but the trial judge let them go to the jury who subsequently convicted both. On appeal it was held that he should not have done so since in the view of the High Court it was plain that 'no reasonable jury could have held that the statements had been voluntary and had not been induced by unfair or improper means'. In so holding the Lord Justice-General observed that:

'It is abundantly clear that the rules of fairness and fair dealing were flagrantly transgressed. I do not say that in no circumstances will a statement by a detainee . . . be inadmissible merely because when it was made he had not received a full caution. What I do say is that the failure of the investigating officers to caution Gray and Tonge in the special circumstances of this case is fatal to the contention that the rules of fair dealing and fairness were properly observed.'

In the circumstances of the case his Lordship was prepared to equiperate the accusations made by the police to the actual reading of a charge. It was a rule of law that the charge had to be preceded by a caution so that the accused was aware of his right to silence and the use that might be made of his response. Thus:

'To charge an accused person without cautioning him is to put pressure upon him which may induce a response and I have no doubt that by accusing Gray, although not in the formal language of a charge, the accusation was clearly calculated, as a formal charge is calculated, to induce a response from the person accused. The accusation placed pressure upon Gray and I am persuaded that since no caution was administered before it was made, it is impossible to regard the statement made in response to it as spontaneous and voluntary. It was plainly induced by the accusation and in the circumstances it was induced by unfair means. It cannot be left out of account either that no caution was administered when the first sentence uttered by Gray made it plain that he intended to make a statement and that no caution was administered when it became obvious that he was about to incriminate himself.'

1 Para 2.81 above.
2 1982 SCCR 313.

**2.97**  Although *Tonge* stopped just short of laying down a firm rule that a statement by a suspect is *ipso facto* inadmissible if he has not been cautioned, it did make it clear that the High Court expects the police to caution a suspect, if not *ab initio*, then certainly when it becomes apparent that he is going to incriminate himself. Any failure to do so will put an incriminating statement at severe risk. However, *Tonge* must now be read subject to *Pennycuik v Lees*[1] (in which *Tonge* was not discussed) in which the High Court retreated slightly from the position which it had previously been thought to have adopted and stated that 'There is no rule of law which requires that a suspect must always be cautioned before any question can be put to him by the police or by anyone else by whom the inquiries are being conducted'. Although this statement is of general application, *Pennycuik* is clearly a case on its own facts and it involved the actions of DSS investigators rather than police officers. The decision can also be justified on the basis that the investigators were only at the preliminary stage of trying to discover whether an offence had been committed and they also required to clarify the identity of the accused. It is undoubtedly difficult to reconcile *Tonge* and *Pennycuik* and it could be argued that a firm rule in favour of cautioning would be easier for the police (or other investigator) to understand and hence fairer to them. If the police are subject to a rule it is surely only reasonable that they should know when they are breaking it. One of the few things which is clear is that it is much less risky for the police to follow the *Tonge* line and caution a suspect before questioning him.

1 1992 SCCR 160.

**2.98** If the suspect has been properly cautioned once, the police are not required to re-caution him each time the questioning moves on to a new matter. Thus, in *Wilson v Heywood*[1] the suspect was cautioned and questioned in relation to one specific incident in relation to which he made an incriminating statement. Thereafter the police, without administering a further caution, questioned him about other matters and further admissions were made. In accordance with 'common practice' the police appear to have cautioned Wilson a second time after he had made these further admissions but before they had been noted, a practice which seems somewhat pointless. In any event, the High Court distinguished *Tonge* without any hesitation on the basis that no caution at all had been given in that case whereas in the instant matter, '. . . before any questioning took place at all he was given a common law caution and was thus aware that he was not obliged to say anything and that anything he did say would be taken down and might be used in evidence'. *Wilson v Heywood* was followed in *Young v Friel*.[2]

1 1989 SLT 279.
2 1992 SCCR 567.

*The fairness test and statutory requirements to give information*

**2.99** There are a limited number of statutory provisions which entitle investigators to require information from people and which may carry a criminal sanction for failure to comply. Whether any incriminating statement is admissible against its maker will depend on the terms of the particular statute. Among these provisions are the

Explosive Substances Act 1883, section 6, Prevention of Terrorism (Temporary Provisions) Act 1976, section 11 and Financial Services Act 1986, section 177.[1]

1 On the latter see *Styr v HM Advocate* 1993 SCCR 278.

**2.100** In relation to the police, by far the most commonly encountered example is section 172 of the Road Traffic Act 1988 which entitles an officer authorised by or on behalf of a chief officer of police to require the person keeping a motor vehicle or 'any other person' to give information as to the identity of the driver of a motor vehicle who is alleged to be guilty of an offence to which the section applies. It is an offence to fail to provide information. A provision of this nature has appeared in successive Road Traffic Acts since 1930 and the relevant section of the 1960 Act was considered in *Foster v Farrell*.[1] In *Foster* the High Court expressly followed the earlier English case of *Bingham v Bruce*.[2] Since the section makes a deep inroad into the general common law principle that a person cannot be compelled to give information which might incriminate him it must be complied with strictly. In *Foster v Farrell* the evidence was held inadmissible because the police officer concerned was not authorised to make the requirement, a point which is much less likely to arise today since virtually all police officers are so authorised. Although the evidence was inadmissible in the circumstances of *Foster*, Lord Justice-Clerk Grant laid down the important principle that information could be required from the driver himself and if it was properly obtained it was admissible in a criminal prosecution against him. His Lordship also had

'no doubt that it is unnecessary to warn or caution a person before requiring him to give information under [this] section. . . . Such a warning or caution would be wholly inappropriate and out of place when the person concerned is bound by statute, and under penal sanction to give the information required.'

1 1963 SLT 182.
2 [1962] 1 All ER 136, [1962] 1 WLR 70.

**2.101** The point about a caution being inappropriate in the context of a statutory requirement was reiterated in *Tudhope v Dalgleish*[1] where the High Court stated bluntly that:

'There is nothing in section 168 [of the Road Traffic Act 1972] dealing with any warning which requires to be given to an individual such as the person keeping the vehicle and nothing regarding any caution which falls to be administered to such individuals. To the contrary, the section is dealing with persons who may be required by the police to give certain information. Accordingly if the Sheriff understood that some form of warning required to be given before information could be required under section 168 the sheriff was in error.'

1  1986 SCCR 559.

**2.102**   It was held in *Duncan v McGillivray*[1] that no specific form of words is necessary for a valid requirement under section 172 and presumably this will apply to other statutory powers to require information.

1  1988 SCCR 488.

**2.103**   In order to make a lawful requirement under section 172 the police officer concerned does not have to be in possession of sufficient evidence to prove the alleged offence. In *Galt v Goodsir*[1] it was held that the section 'ought to be construed to mean . . . that the essential prerequisite to the exercise of the statutory power is an allegation of an offence by the driver, made in good faith, and based on information indicating as a probability, that that offence has been committed.'

1  1981 SCCR 225.

**2.104**   *Galt v Goodsir* is also authority for the proposition that in the situation where only one police officer has seen the accused driving, it is unobjectionable for that officer to make a section 172 requirement in the presence of a colleague who had not seen the driving specifically in order to obtain corroboration. The same point was made in *Whiteside v Scott*.[1]

1  Unreported, CO Circular A22/91.

**2.105**   The police may only use the section 172 power where the offence alleged against the driver is one to which the section applies, essentially offences against the Road Traffic Acts and other legislation relating to the use of vehicles on roads. Thus if it is alleged that a driver had been guilty of a common law offence such as theft or assault or a contravention of a non-road traffic enactment, for example the Misuse of Drugs Act 1971, the police have no right to invoke section 172. On the other hand even if they are entitled to do so the police are not obliged to use the statutory power and if they do not the admissibility of an incriminatory statement by the owner or driver of a motor vehicle will fall to be determined by the normal common law rules as was held in *Miln v Cullen*.[1]

1  1967 JC 21.

**2.106**   The High Court will place a strict interpretation on statutory provisions derogating from the right to silence and the court will also be concerned to ensure that the privilege against self-incrimination is not eroded except by the clearest and most express statutory provision. This is well illustrated by the opinion of Lord Ross in *HM Advocate v Von.*[1] In this case the accused had been questioned while detained under the Prevention of Terrorism Act 1976. Section 11 of this Act penalised a person who failed 'without reasonable excuse' to disclose information about acts of terrorism to the police. There was no express provision dealing with the admissibility of any incriminatory statement. The police had neither cautioned Von nor otherwise informed him that he was not required to incriminate himself. They had also failed to bring to his attention the 'without reasonable excuse' proviso. Lord Ross excluded the resulting statement observing:

'I do not consider that a statement can be regarded as being fairly obtained if the accused was never advised of the fact that under our law no person is required to incriminate himself. In enacting the provisions of the Act of 1976, if parliament had intended to make statements of suspects admissible against them in the event of their being subsequently charged I would have expected parliament to have made that clear. I cannot believe that parliament intended to alter the well-established principle of our law that no man can be compelled to incriminate himself. . . . No doubt statements may be taken from suspects under the Act, and such statements may assist the police in their inquiries; but they will not in my opinion be admissible against a suspect who is subsequently charged unless the suspect has been advised that he cannot be compelled to implicate himself.'

1 1979 SLT (Notes) 62.

*Fairness and statements made in relation to other matters*

**2.107** It has previously been noted that no clear rule has emerged to deal with the admissibility of a declaration emitted in respect of a charge different from that which eventually appeared on the indictment. The point first arose in relation to statements to the police in *HM Advocate v Cunningham.*[1] The accused had been charged with assault to danger of life and had made an incriminating statement. The victim subsequently died and Cunningham was indicted for murder. Interestingly, the trial judge, Lord Moncrieff, went against the only comparable earlier authority[2] and admitted the statement holding that the death of the victim did not affect the relevancy or materiality of the statement which had been made in response to a grave charge. Shortly thereafter the reverse situation arose in *Willis v HM Advocate*[3] where a statement made in relation to a charge of murder was admitted in a trial for culpable homicide. On appeal the High Court had no difficulty in holding that since the statement had been made in relation to the more serious charge, which included the lesser one, it had been correctly admitted. *Cunningham* was only a single judge decision and in *HM Advocate v Graham*,[4] a case of capital murder, Lord Sorn took the opposite view from Lord Moncrieff and refused to admit a statement made when the accused had been charged with assault causing grievous bodily harm (sic). His Lordship considered that if on the earlier occasion he had been charged with capital murder he might have been more careful in what he said or indeed might have preferred to hold his tongue altogether.

1 1939 JC 61.
2 *James Stewart* (1866) 5 Irv 31.
3 1941 JC 1.
4 1958 SLT 167.

**2.108**  This conflict of authority was finally resolved in *McAdam v HM Advocate*.[1] In this case the accused had originally been charged by the police with assault to severe injury but was indicted for attempted murder. He was convicted and on appeal it was argued that his reply to the original charge ought not to have been admitted, defence counsel contending that a statement in reply to a lesser charge was not admissible in relation to a more serious crime. Lord Justice-General Clyde refused to accept counsel's argument that a reply was only admissible if the original charge was identical to that on the indictment since that conflicted with *Willis* which had already laid down that a statement in reply to a more serious charge was admissible where the trial was for a lesser charge. His Lordship pointed out that in almost every case the full facts are not known to the police when the original charge is made and it would be unreasonable to exclude from the jury's consideration a reply to the theft of four articles merely because the accused was later indicted for stealing five. The High Court laid down two general considerations which must be kept in view: (i) the evidence can only be admitted if the crime charged on each of the two occasions falls into a single category – both must be crimes inferring dishonesty or inferring personal violence; and (ii) each of the charges must substantially cover the same *species facti*. It was stressed in *McAdam* that the facts should be substantially similar (as opposed to identical) since the full extent of the theft or of the victim's injuries might not have been discovered at the time the charge was made. Where this was the case, justice demanded that the jury be informed of the reply made to the original limited charge. It followed that if the original charge was assault and the indictment alleged aggravated assault, which Lord Clyde considered included culpable homicide and non-capital murder, the reply to the original charge could be proved provided the *species facti* in both charges was substantially the same. An *obiter* observation indicated that the High Court might have been prepared to consider the possibility of a different rule in the case of capital murder but the point never arose in the few years which remained before the death penalty was abolished.

1 1960 SLT 47.

*The accused's understanding and the fairness test*

**2.109** If the court is not satisfied that the accused was fully and rationally aware of what he was doing when he made an incriminatory statement, the fairness test will be likely to lead to the statement being excluded. The same result may well follow if it appears that the statement was made when the accused was under some form of misapprehension. Much will depend (as always) on individual circumstances and only illustrative examples can be given.

**2.110** In *McClory v MacInness*[1] it was held that a statement was unfairly obtained from a suspect when plain-clothes police officers wakened him from sleep and without caution asked him 'What happened?' This was clearly a question designed to elicit a reply.

1 1992 SCCR 319.

**2.111** In *HM Advocate v Lieser*[1] the accused had been charged with murder and was still in the charge room. The policeman who had been talking to him addressed a question to a colleague. Lieser mistakenly thought the question had been addressed to him and made a reply which was presumably incriminating. Lord Constable considered the point on the borderline but decided to disallow evidence of the reply.

1 1926 JC 88.

**2.112** *HM Advocate v McSwiggan*[1] is an extraordinary case and among other problems the spectre of the judicial declaration arose to confuse the issue. McSwiggan had been arrested and detained on a charge of incest with his sister, who had become pregnant. While he was in custody a police officer took him out of his cell and asked him some general questions about his family and personal circumstances. Without any prompting by the policeman, McSwiggan started to explain how he could not be reponsible for his sister's pregnancy. The officer cautioned him and told him not to speak about the matter but he insisted. Another officer was summoned and he also cautioned McSwiggan but nevertheless he went ahead and made a signed statement detailing how he had had intercourse with his sister and the precautions he had taken to avoid getting her pregnant. The accused appears to have been not very bright and one of the police officers said that he gathered the accused thought that there was no crime if there was no child. At the trial objection was taken to the evidence of the statement on various grounds including the absence of a solicitor and the accused's misunderstanding of the true nature of the charge. The defence also argued that the statement should have been made before a magistrate. The Crown argued that the statement was admissible having been voluntarily made after due warning and it had to be presumed that the accused knew it was a criminal offence to have intercourse with his sister. However, the trial judge rejected the evidence despite finding that the statement had been voluntarily made and the conduct of the police had been suitable and proper. In his view the police should have refused to hear McSwiggan's statement and taken him before a magistrate to emit a declaration, this despite judicial examination having long been an empty shell. Remarkably, the trial judge also took the view that, since the accused was unaware of the true nature of the crime with which he was charged, he had not been adequately warned with regard to the making of the statement and the statement was thus inadmissible. This decision has been trenchantly criticised[2] and it is doubtful whether it would be followed today.

1 1937 JC 50.
2 A D Gibb 'Fair Play for the Criminal' (1954) 66 JR 199.

**2.113** If the accused is not a native English speaker, it is self-evident that his command of the language will be a factor for consideration in deciding whether any statement has been fairly obtained. Thus in *HM Advocate v Olsson*[1] Lord Jamieson refused to admit a statement made without an interpreter by a Swedish sailor since the accused had only a limited command of English and the court could not be satisfied either that he had understood the caution which he had been given or that the police had properly understood what he had been trying to say to them. In modern practice, a trial judge will only be entitled to withhold a statement from a jury if it is clear that no reasonable jury could hold that the statement had been fairly obtained. Otherwise the ability of the accused to speak and understand English will simply become a matter for the jury to take into consideration in determining whether the statement was fairly obtained in the circumstances of the individual case.[2]

1 1941 JC 63.
2 *Montes v HM Advocate* 1990 SCCR 645 at 672–673 per Lord Weir.

**2.114** Similarly, the accused's mental capacity or the level of his intelligence is generally regarded as only one of the factors for the jury to consider in determining the overall issue of fairness. However, if the statement has clearly been obtained unfairly, even by inadvertence, it will be inadmissible. Thus, in *HM Advocate v Gilgannon*[1] the accused was medically examined while in police custody and found to be, in the opinion of the police doctor, mentally subnormal and unable to give a clear account of the incident in connection with which he was in custody. For some reason this finding does not appear to have been communicated to the police officers who took a voluntary statement from the accused some four-and-a-half hours after the examination. At any rate, no steps were taken to ascertain whether he was fit to make the statement. There was no question of the police resorting to improper threats or bullying but Lord Cameron held the statement inadmissible. His Lordship was clear that the court should look at the circumstances in which the statement was taken as well as the manner in which it was obtained and elicited.

1 1983 SCCR 10.

**2.115** *Gilgannon* was distinguished in *Higgins v HM Advocate*[1] where one of the accused, Grogan, was mentally ill, having suffered from schizophrenia for some five years. The medical evidence at the trial indicated that he had been of diminished responsibility at the time of the crime but it also indicated that while in police custody he had been orientated in all senses, apart from getting the date wrong, and he was fit to plead. A distinguished forensic psychiatrist who gave evidence said that Grogan suffered from delusions, and being mentally ill could be suggestible, and he also pointed out that in assessing the reliability of what he said it was necessary to bear in mind that he was suffering from schizophrenia. Nevertheless, the trial judge left the issue of fairness to the jury and on appeal it was held that he was correct to do so.

1 1993 SCCR 542.

**2.116** It is possibly surprising that there is an almost complete absence of authority on the fairness of statements obtained from persons under the influence of drink or drugs. Presumably, unless the matter is so clearly unfair that the judge is justified in excluding the statement, the level of intoxication will merely become yet another factor for the jury to consider. The only relevant case, *Thomson v HM Advocate*[1] held that there was no issue of fairness in the taking of a statement from an accused who had consumed alcohol but was not unaware of his actions.

1 1989 SLT 170.

## *The fairness test and overheard statements*

**2.117** So far this discussion has only considered the issue of statements specifically made to police officers but it will be apparent that there can be circumstances in which police officers, whether deliberately or inadvertently, overhear incriminatory statements which were not intended for their ears. The law on this point is still not entirely fixed but in relation to shouted conversations between prisoners in police stations a conflict of authority between the old single-judge High Court case of *HM Advocate v Keen*[1] and the decision of Sheriff MacPhail in *HM Advocate v O'Donnell*[2] has now been resolved in favour of the latter. Although *Keen* has never actually been overruled, it is clearly an aberration, being contrary to earlier authority when it was decided,[3] and it can safely be said that it no longer represents the law.

1  1926 JC 1.
2  1975 SLT (Sh Ct) 22.
3  *Robert Brown* (1833) Bell's Notes 244; *James Miller* (1837) Bell's Notes 244; *John Johnston* (1845) 2 Broun 401.

**2.118**  The modern law now rests on *Jamieson v Annan*.[1] In this case police officers had overheard a shouted conversation of an incriminating nature between two accused persons who had been cautioned and charged and detained in separate cells in a police station. It appears that one of the officers had accidentally overheard the start of the conversation and had then brought in other officers to listen to what was said. The High Court expressly approved Sheriff MacPhail's judgment in *O'Donnell* and applied the test of bilateral fairness, holding that what had been said had been entirely voluntary and without inducement or trap. *Jamieson v Annan* settles the basic issue of the conversation overheard entirely accidentally. At the other extreme any trap or inducement by the police will be likely to lead to the statement being excluded.[2] Nevertheless a grey area still exists and it remains to be seen what view the High Court will take if the police know or suspect that accused persons will try to communicate with each other and, for example, place officers in the cell passage specifically for the purpose of listening out and recording anything that is said. Professor A D Gibb stated the obvious when he commented that 'Men in police stations who shout their observations must surely be taken to know that policemen will hear them'[3] and *Dickson*[4] was of the view that conversations picked up by eavesdropping were admissible. Although it is impossible to be certain, it is thought that under modern conditions any statement overheard in this manner would be admissible provided the police themselves did nothing to induce the conversation. However, difficult issues could arise, for example the possibility of prisoners deliberately being placed in separate cells to make their conversations audible to the police, and each case will require to be determined on its own facts and any concessions which the police are prepared to make in relation to their own conduct.

1 1988 SLT (Notes) 631.
2 Cf *HM Advocate v Anderson* 1980 SLT (Notes) 104.
3 'Fair Play for the Criminal' 1954 JR 199.
4 Page 243, § 348.

**2.119** Apart from shouted conversations in police stations, the situation can arise that the police may arrange to overhear a conversation between a suspect and a third party who is not a police officer in the hope that incriminating statements are made. There are two single-judge decisions dealing with this issue and both are against admission of the resulting evidence.

**2.120** Firstly, in *HM Advocate v Campbell*,[1] a case of murder, the accused had telephoned a newspaper and asked a reporter to meet him in a public house so that he could make a statement, apparently with a view to obtaining payment. He said that the reporter was not to bring the police with him. The paper nonetheless informed the police and a police officer disguised as a second reporter went to the meeting. The accused brought with him a pair of bloodstained trousers which he handed over to the disguised policeman. The accused again raised the question of payment and the 'real' reporter assured him that payment would be forthcoming although no amount was agreed. He then made a statement which the reporter took down, asking a few questions to clear up some ambiguities. After the statement had been made, and had presumably been incriminating, the policeman, who up to this point had taken no part in the proceedings, identified himself and cautioned the accused. At the trial, objection was taken to the admissibility of the statement. The trial judge dealt with the matter shortly, holding that the accused had to be treated as being under suspicion at the time the statement was made. The sole purpose of the policeman being there was to hear the statement and in the circumstances there was a duty on him to warn or caution the accused before the statement was made.

1 1964 JC 80.

**2.121** The present writer would respectfully suggest that this case was wrongly decided. Just as people who shout out incriminating remarks in a police station must be taken to accept the possibility of policemen overhearing, surely people who voluntarily offer to sell stories of their murderous activities to the press must be taken to accept the possibility of the police being tipped off. The statement would surely have been admissible if the reporter had simply gone along on his own. The policeman in this case did nothing to induce the statement, and acted merely as a passive observer of a course of conduct on which the accused had already embarked.

**2.122** It is also difficult to see any logic to the apparent distinction between the situation where the police overhear the actual offence being committed and the situation where they overhear the accused telling someone that he has been responsible. In *Hopes and Lavery v HM Advocate*[1] the police used a radio transmitter and a tape-recorder to overhear and record a conversation between a blackmailer and his victim. The resulting evidence was held admissible, Lord Justice-General Clyde observing, 'It hardly lies in the mouth of a blackmailer to complain that the jury are told the truth about his conversations, when he is exerting pressure on his cornered victim. His remedy is not to blackmail'. The same can be said about a murderer who volunteers to sell information to the press. His remedy is not to murder, or at the very least not to try to make money from his crime. The decision in *Campbell* also conflicts with decisions reached elsewhere in the United Kingdom around the same time. In *R v Masqsud Ali, R v Ashiq Hussain*[2] it was observed by Marshall J that 'The criminal does not act according to the Queensberry Rules. The method of the informer and of the eavesdropper is commonly used in the detection of crime'. Similarly, in *R v Murphy*[3] it was pointed out that 'Detection by deception is a form of police procedure to be directed and used sparingly and with circumspection; but as a method it is as old as the constable in plain clothes . . .'.[4]

1 1960 JC 104.
2 [1965] 2 All ER 464.
3 [1965] NI 138.
4 See also *Cross on Evidence* (7th edn) p 486.

**2.123** The other Scottish single-judge decision, *HM Advocate v Graham*,[1] has many similarities to *Campbell*, which was considered in argument. Graham was a suspect who had previously been interviewed under caution by the police. It came to their notice that he was going to have a meeting with a civilian, R, on matters which were likely to be relevant to the police inquiry. The information appears to have come from R himself and he was 'wired up' with a radio transmitter. The meeting took place and certain incriminating statements were apparently made and recorded by the police. It appears that after the meeting was over, R himself introduced certain topics into the conversation and this resulted in the most important admissions being made. The trial judge ruled the admissions inadmissible which resulted in the Crown having to withdraw the indictment. His Lordship considered that since Graham was a suspect:

'If such questions had been put at that time by police officers in the course of interrogation of the panel without due caution, statements made in response to them would have been inadmissible. I can see no reason why such statements should be rendered admissible by the fact that they were secured by a third party, not a police officer, where the third party asks them in the knowledge that he is being overheard by police officers concerned in an enquiry into the matters about which he is asking questions, and who has been provided by the police with equipment to enable them to overhear what passes. . . . In principle I see no distinction between a case such as the present one where the third party is provided by the police officers investigating the crime with a list of questions to ask the suspect in the hope of securing admissions of guilt, or the example of inadmissible evidence cited in *Macdonald on the Criminal Law of Scotland* (5th edn) p 314 where an official procures a fellow prisoner to inveigle the accused into conversation to be overheard by the official, which last could only be regarded as entrapment.'

1 1991 SCCR 56.

**2.124** As Sheriff Gordon has pointed out, the decision in *Graham* seems to set a special standard for the police and it is difficult to defend its logic:

'Indeed it may depend on [the statements] having been obtained specifically by police deception which would suggest that the aim of the law is to ensure that the police act like gentlemen. It is unlikely that the statements would have been rejected if R had acted off his own bat, without any police involvement at all, but with the intention of obtaining evidence from the accused which he could present to the police. But the accused might feel just as "fooled" by that situation as by one in which R was acting with the connivance of the police.'

**2.125** Given the importance of the point, it is slightly surprising that the Crown did not seek a Lord Advocate's Reference to review the decision in *Graham*. However in *Weir v Jessop (No 2)*[1] *Campbell* was the subject of express, though *obiter*, disapproval and the soundness of *Graham* was implicitly doubted. It would appear probable that once this issue eventually reaches the appeal court, an overheard statement to a third party will be held admissible, at least to the extent of passing the 'no reasonable jury' test, provided the police have done nothing to induce the accused to make the statement or to follow a course of action which he would not otherwise have done.

1 1991 SCCR 636.

*Fairness and the statement which constitutes the offence*

**2.126**   The fairness test as it has been discussed here does not fall to be applied in the unusual situation where the statement to the police itself constitutes the offence. In *Tung Wang Ming v HM Advocate*[1] the accused, a Chinese restauranteur, had gone to the police station following the arrest of one of his employees. There was some dubiety about the employee's true name and while this was being discussed the accused offered the police officers bribes in the form of free meals and money to secure the employee's release. The police warned him of his position but the only effect of the warning was to increase the sum of money on offer! One of the officers sought the advice of a superior and the superior and another officer listened from a concealed position while the accused was again asked the name of the employee, whereupon he offered all the money in his pocket for his release. The concealed officers then revealed themselves and the accused was cautioned and charged. In this situation Sheriff A G Johnston explicitly directed the jury that they were not to consider the issue of whether what the police did was fair or not and on appeal he was upheld. The High Court stressed that at the material time Tung was not in the position of an accused or a suspect, and was not being questioned about his own alleged guilt of any offence. The evidence of what the accused said was evidence of the crime itself.

1  1987 SCCR 110.

# EXTRA-JUDICIAL CONFESSIONS – PERSONS OTHER THAN THE POLICE

## Prison officers

**2.127**   In the texts prison officers have generally been assimilated to police officers for the purpose of determining the admissibility of confessions or admissions made to them.[1] However, there is a dearth of modern authority, the point not having arisen this century. *Hume* disapproved strongly of any confession by a person in prison being received in evidence[2] and historically the courts have been very careful to ensure that no person who had the custody of a prisoner abused his or her position of influence over the prisoner.[3] In one very unusual case, *Janet Hope or Walker*,[4] the keeper of the prison had become in effect a religious adviser and confidant of the accused and in the course of his conversations with her she had made certain admissions. The evidence of these was rejected at the trial although the court made it clear that the case was 'very special' and was not to be taken as laying down a precedent.

1 *Dickson* p 240, § 344; *Walker and Walker* p 38, § 41; *Renton and Brown* para 18–38.
2 II, 335–336.
3 See *Catherine Beaton or Bethune* (1856) 2 Irv 457; *May Grant* (1862) 4 Irv 183; *HM Advocate v Proudfoot* (1882) 4 Coup 590.
4 (1845) 2 Broun 465.

**2.128**  On the basis of nineteenth-century authority it would appear that a prison officer should caution the accused and any statement which was elicited by questions (and presumably by any other form of unfairness) runs the risk of being held inadmissible.[1] However, it must be doubted whether the statement in the current edition of *Renton and Brown*[2] that 'prison officers should probably not receive confessions at all, but send for a magistrate or perhaps for the police' is in accordance with modern views. It is thought that the courts would apply the normal modern criterion of bilateral fairness and it must be considered highly unlikely that a truly voluntary statement to a prison officer would be rejected on the basis that he had not sent for the police, let alone a magistrate.

1 *Macdonald* p 314, following *HM Advocate v Proudfoot* (1882) 4 Coup 590; *MacPhail* § 20.18.
2 Para 18–39.

### Fellow prisoners

**2.129**  Despite *Hume's* disapproval, it has long been established that a confession made by a prisoner to a person confined along with him is admissible, provided that the person to whom he makes it has not been induced to converse with him by anybody connected with the prosecution.[1] This would appear to apply irrespective of whether evidence of the conversation is given by the fellow prisoner or by a prison official who has overheard the conversation. In the latter case the same rules would appear to apply as do in the case of police officers.[2]

1 Eg *Robert Emond* (1830) Bell's Notes 243; *Wm Wright* (1835) 1 Swin 6; *James Miller* (1837) Bell's Notes 244; *Alison* II, 584; *Dickson* p 243, § 348.
2 *Renton and Brown* para 18–40; cf *Robert Brown* (1833) Bell's Notes 244.

### Public officials and investigators other than the police

**2.130**  There have been a number of cases involving statements to persons acting in official or quasi-official capacities. Many of the older authorities are of little more than curiosity value today. Thus *Hume*

quotes with disapproval some early examples of confessions to magistrates, an Advocate Depute and the Solicitor General being accepted
in evidence.[1] The earliest example of a confession to an official being
rejected is *Alexander Robertson and Elizabeth Bennet*[2] in which certain
admissions relating to the paternity of an incestuous child made to an
inspector of the poor were held inadmissible on the basis that they had
been obtained by undue influence. This was followed by *Philip Turner
and Peter Rennie*[3] when the court expressed doubt as to the
competency of evidence of a statement by a naval rating to a superior
officer on the ground that the statement could not be said to be voluntary, the rating being under a duty to give his commander a full
account of anything which occurred during the time he was on duty.
The point was not pressed and later in the same case the court
sustained an objection that a statement to the procurator fiscal (who
had come on board the ship for the purpose of making inquiries) was a
precognition and hence not evidence.

1 II, 335–336.
2 (1853) 1 Irv 219.
3 (1853) 1 Irv 284.

**2.131**  The later case of *Waddell v Kinnaird*[1] can also be seen as
falling into this category, since the accused railwayman was questioned
by his stationmaster, albeit in front of two police officers, and indeed
the magistrate held that the conversation was a business conversation
outwith the strictly criminal investigation and the majority of the
appeal court agreed with him. Lord Ormidale's strong dissent has
already been noted[2] and it is considered by some commentators that
his dissenting judgment would now be followed.[3] However, the
dissent was on the basis that the presence of the police made the
stationmaster's questioning a police inquiry and Lord Ormidale
expressed no views on the propriety of such questioning in the
absence of the police, although he did not accept the idea that it was
simply 'a business conversation' since the accused, being a mere lamp-
man, would normally be under a duty to reply to questions from the
stationmaster.

1 1922 JC 40.
2 Para 2.34 above.
3 *Walker and Walker* p 37, § 40; *MacPhail* § 20.19.

**2.132**  In *Morrison v Burrell*[1] Lord Justice-General Cooper drew a
clear distinction between an investigation by the police addressed to a
citizen charged with or detained on suspicion of a crime and a 'dom-
estic investigation' by officials of a public department into irregula-
rities in the conduct of a public service. His Lordship upheld a decision

to admit statements made under caution by the accused post-master to questions from post office investigators who appear to have had in their minds a strong suspicion that he had breached post office regulations but only a possibility of his conduct having been fraudulent. In the circumstances his Lordship held that there was an 'absence of any hint or trace of impropriety, unfairness or mis-use by the investigators of their position – a factor of vital importance in all cases of this kind'.

1  1947 JC 43.

**2.133** Somewhat surprisingly there has been no reported decision on an 'internal' investigation since *Morrison v Burrell* and there is a remarkable dearth of recent reported authority on the permissible limits of interrogation by 'security officers' and senior colleagues. However, the general fairness test will now fall to be applied by the trial court as can be seen from *McCuiag v Annan*[1] and if the behaviour of the investigator is unfair the statement will be excluded. Thus in one unreported case, *Mackay v Smith*,[2] a summary conviction was quashed where post office investigators had pressed the suspect to give answers which 'they were quite evidently determined to get'.

1  1986 SCCR 535; para 2.135 below.
2  High Court, August 1977, unreported; see Gordon *Admissibility* p 343.

**2.134**  *HM Advocate v Friel*[1] concerned the questioning by officers of Customs and Excise of a person suspected of VAT and income tax offences. The questioning began as part of a routine inquiry with the accused not being suspected of any specific offence and a possibility that he could have exculpated himself if he had given satisfactory answers. However, suspicion of specific offences did come to focus on him and although he was cautioned he was subjected to sustained and forceful questioning involving repeated and searching questions which were pressed on him. Lord Ross applied the fairness test and refused to admit evidence of the accused's reply to this questioning. His Lordship quoted with approval Lord Cooper's observation in *Chalmers* to the effect that interrogation would have the effect of making the accused a compellable witness at his own trial. It would accordingly appear that revenue officials are subject to the same general principles as apply to the police.

1  1978 SLT (Notes) 21.

**2.135**  *McCuaig v Annan*[1] was a straightforward example of a shop manager catching a shoplifter who had left the shop in possession of stolen property. He asked the accused to return to the store which she did voluntarily. The manager then summoned another member of staff and in her presence asked the accused (a) why she had taken the stolen items, to which she replied that a friend had told her to and (b) whether she had anything else she had not paid for, to which she replied that she had not. When the manager said he was going to phone the police the accused became tearful and offered to pay for the stolen items. When the police arrived, one officer without cautioning the accused asked her why she had taken the property and she again answered that a friend had told her to. The justices at the trial held that there had been no cross-examination, duress or undue pressure from the store manager and the evidence of the admission to him was fairly obtained and accordingly admissible. The justices also made the point that civilian store employees could not be expected to know how to administer a caution. However, the statement to the police was held inadmissible on the basis that the accused was clearly a suspected person and should have been cautioned before being questioned. On appeal the decision to admit the statement to the manager was upheld. Lord Justice-Clerk Ross observed:

'No doubt when one is considering whether or not to admit evidence of questions of this kind, the general test of fairness will fall to be implied (sic). Mr G however was not a police officer, and as the justices point out in their note he could not be expected to be aware of how to administer a caution. . . . Equally it is not surprising in the circumstances that he should have thought it appropriate to address some questions to her regarding the matter. Whether or not the questions put and the actings of Mr G were fair was a matter for the justices to determine.'

*McCuaig* is only of importance in that it deals with, and clarifies, an everyday situation, and while the Lord Justice-Clerk was at pains to stress that the decision on fairness (and hence admissibility) was one for the justices, the High Court would, nevertheless, have intervened if the justices had misdirected themselves.[2]

1 1986 SCCR 535.
2 Cf *Heywood v Smith* 1989 SCCR 391.

**2.136** In *Irving v Tudhope*[1] two officials specifically employed to investigate television licence evasion called at the appellant's house. They were aware that she did not appear on the current list of licence holders and on obtaining entry to her house they observed a television set in operation. Without cautioning her they asked whether she held a licence and she admitted that she did not. In upholding the conviction the High Court referred to *McCuaig v Annan* and pointed out that there was nothing to show that the officials even knew how to administer a caution. In any event there was no question of them trying to provoke an incriminating reply. The earlier case of *Walkingshaw v McIntyre*[2] was overruled.

1 1987 SCCR 505.
2 1985 SCCR (Sh Ct) 389.

**2.137** While the actual decision to uphold the conviction in *Irving v Tudhope* is entirely consistent with cases such as *Custerson v Westwater*[1] and *Wingate v Mackinnon*[2] it seems to the writer that as a matter of principle officials who are employed by the agencies of the state for the specific purpose of investigating whether members of the public are breaking the law are in a rather different category from shop managers or senior employees in a commercial undertaking, who may go for a lifetime without ever coming across criminal conduct. There would appear to be an argument for saying that all state investigators and enforcement officers should be assimilated to the police (and apparently nowadays revenue officers) and should be subject to the same legal requirements with regard to cautioning and fairness generally. In *Lawrie v Muir*,[3] a case dealing with an illegal search carried out by milk inspectors, Lord Cooper commented that such inspectors 'ought to know the precise limits of their authority' and this remark would seem to be equally appropriate in the context of questioning. However, there are no Scottish decisions on statements to non-police investigators beyond the stage of preliminary enquiry and the point cannot be regarded as anything other than wide open.

1 1987 SCCR 389.
2 High Court, 13 June 1989, unreported, CO Circular A27/89.
3 1950 JC 19.

**2.138** Non-police state investigators may enjoy special statutory powers to require information or to require a suspect to answer questions and/or produce documents. These powers may result in a drastic curtailment of the right to silence although in every case it is necessary to refer to the specific terms of the statute concerned to see precisely what is authorised.[1] In some cases the statute may provide that any resulting statement is inadmissible against its maker but even if the statement is admissible in terms of the statute the Scottish courts will still apply the fairness test when considering whether it should be received.[2] The following examples are simply illustrative of the various forms of statutory powers to require information and are in no way exhaustive.

1 See generally J D Heydon 'Statutory Restrictions on the Privilege Against Self Incrimination' (1971) 87 LQR 214 and Mirfield *Confessions* pp 92–93.
2 *Styr v HM Advocate* 1993 SCCR 278.

**2.139**   Under section 434 of the Companies Act 1985 a Department of Trade and Industry inspector who is investigating the affairs of a company may require officers and agents of the company to attend before him, produce relevant books and documents and 'otherwise give . . . all assistance in connection with the investigation which they are reasonably able to give'. The inspector may examine on oath, and a person who fails to attend, to produce documents or to answer questions is liable to be held in contempt of court.[1] Moreover, any answer which is given to the inspector may be used in evidence against the maker. Similar provisions may be found in sections 177 and 178 of the Financial Services Act 1986 where the inspector is investigating 'insider dealing'. In *Styr v HM Advocate*[2] the High Court followed the English case of *R v Director of Serious Fraud Office ex parte Smith*[3] and held that section 177 overrode the principle that a witness was not bound to answer a question which would incriminate him, since section 177(6) expressly provided that a statement could be used in evidence against the person making it. However, the test of fairness still applied in determining whether evidence was admissible at a criminal trial. It was also held that in view of the terms of section 177 it would have been inappropriate for a caution to be administered.

1 See J Plumptre 'The Right of Silence Disappears' (1989) 139 New LJ 1070.
2 1993 SCCR 278.
3 [1992] 3 WLR 66.

**2.140**   By contrast, section 2 of the Criminal Justice Act 1987 permits the Director of the Serious Fraud Office or a person authorised by him to require a person under investigation to attend before him and answer questions or otherwise furnish information with respect to any matter relevant to the investigation. However, a statement so made is only admissible in evidence against the maker if he gives evidence inconsistent with it or if he is prosecuted under section 2(14) for making a false statement.

**2.141**   Section 20(2)(j) of the Health and Safety at Work Etc Act 1974 empowers an inspector under that Act to require any person whom he has reasonable cause to believe to be able to give information relevant to any examination or investigation within the inspector's field of responsibility to answer such questions as the inspector may think fit to ask, and the inspector may also require a person to sign a declaration of the truth of his answers. However, section 20(7) expressly provides that no answer given under section 20(2)(j) shall be admissible in evidence against the person giving it or their husband or wife.

**2.142**   There is no Scottish authority dealing with the admissibility of a statement made to an official possessed of a power to require information but who does not exercise his power. Such a situation might arise if an employer volunteered or blurted out an incriminatory statement to a factory inspector investigating an accident. *Prima facie* such a statement would appear to be admissible in the event of the prosecution of its maker on an analogy with cases such as *Smith v Lamb*.[1]

1   (1888) 15 R(J) 54; para 2.31 above.


## Private persons

**2.143**   Once again the task of stating the law on this topic is complicated by the absence of modern authority and also a degree of confusion as to the definition of a 'private' person. *Hume*[1] lists a number of cases from as early as 1663 where confessions to private persons have been accepted in evidence. As he points out such confessions are frequently so interwoven with the other facts and circumstances of the case that they 'cannot without violence be separated from them; nor the witnesses give their evidence intelligibly, or with the due connection, without relating this part of the story also'. In none of the cases to which he refers was any pressure apparently brought to bear on the accused to confess.

1   II, 333–334.


**2.144**   *Alison*[1] argues that confessions to private persons are admissible even if made 'on a promise of safety or protection from the injured party or anyone else', provided the person making the promise is not connected with the prosecutor. The latter category he restricts to 'the public prosecutor or any person identified with him as the Procurator Fiscal, Sheriff, Clerk of Court, or the like'. Thus, he says, nothing is more common than for a prisoner to confess, upon an understanding, express or implied, to the party injured that he is not to be prosecuted. Such a confession is, according to *Alison*, admissible provided the assurance of safety is given by 'the private party only, or an officious third person, as a constable or sheriff-officer, or the like' such, apparently, not being regarded as 'identified' with the public prosecutor. While *Alison* concedes that such inducements could well affect the weight of the evidence with the jury, he justifies his argument on the basis 'that it is not in the power of a private party, by any promises or indiscretions on his part to tie up the hands, or restrain the proof of the public prosecutor'.

1   *Practice* p 581.

**2.145**  *Alison*'s argument, on closer inspection, turns out to be based on one case only,[1] where the promise of safety came from the manager of premises which had suffered a housebreaking. It is thought that *Alison*'s view of constables and sheriff officers was incorrect and it was doubted by *Dickson*.[2] Apart from this point, however, *Dickson* largely follows *Alison*'s reasoning that inducement by a private person not connected with the prosecution does not render a confession inadmissible.[3] *Macdonald*, quoting *Dickson*, simply states that 'Statements made to private individuals cannot be objected to, even although made in answer to questions, provided they are not extracted'.[4]

1 *Honeyman and Smith* (1815) Hume II 335.
2 Page 240, § 344.
3 Page 242, §§ 345–346.
4 Page 315.

**2.146**  The only writers to question this view are *Walker and Walker* who state:

'The view has been expressed that confessions are equally admissible in evidence, even if made as the result of *threats*, *undue influence* or inducements by persons not associated with the judiciary, prosecutor or police. The decisions, however, do not uniformly support this view. It is thought that fundamentally the matter is one of fairness to the accused and the likelihood or otherwise that the inducement or threat resulted in the making of a false confession.'[1]

Although the words in italics have occasionally been used in cases[2] neither *Alison* nor *Dickson* to whom *Walker and Walker* attribute this view actually made any reference to threats or undue influence. *Walker and Walker* refer to three cases which in their opinion 'do not uniformly support this view'[3] but all these cases involve persons acting in, at least, a quasi-official capacity and in one, *HM Advocate v Graham*,[4] the circumstances were quite extraordinary, involving a town councillor offering a prisoner a reward of £100 for information leading to the recovery of stolen property. Part of the difficulty at least appears to stem from a failure to define firstly what is meant by a 'private individual' and secondly what constitutes a threat.

1 Page 37, § 40, emphasis added.
2 Eg *HM Advocate v Parker* 1944 JC 49.
3 *Alexander Robertson and Elizabeth Bennet* (1853) 1 Irv 219; *Philip Turner and Peter Rennie* (1853) 1 Irv 284; and *HM Advocate v Graham* (1876) 3 Coup 217.
4 Above.

**2.147**  In modern practice it would appear on the basis of cases such as *McCuaig v Annan*[1] that the fairness test will be applied today and, as Lord Cameron has put it:

'[A] confession to a private party will be admissible unless the circumstances in which it has been made or extracted are such as to raise doubt as to whether it has been falsely made in order to escape from further pressure or in response to inducements offered, and that this is an issue which is essentially for the jury to determine upon the evidence laid before them.'[2]

1 1986 SCCR 535.
2 1975 SLT (News) 265 at 268.

**2.148**  It scarcely needs to be said that any attempt by the police to use a private person to obtain a confession which would be inadmissible if obtained by the police themselves would result in the confession being rendered inadmissible.[1]

1 Cf *Mahler and Berrenhard* (1857) 2 Irv 634; *Waddell v Kinnaird* 1922 JC 40; *HM Advocate v Campbell* 1964 JC 80.

**2.149**  From the few cases that there have been it seems clear that confessions to friends or relatives are admissible even if the result of questioning, provided they have not been extracted by unfair means.[1] Thus, in *HM Advocate v Parker*[2] a statement by the accused to his brother while in prison on a charge of murder was admitted against him. The general rule is, of course, subject to the statutory provision which lays down that the spouse of an accused, though competent, is not a compellable witness for the prosecution.[3]

1 *Renton and Brown* paras 18–47, 18–48.
2 1944 JC 49.
3 Criminal Procedure (Scotland) Act 1975, ss 143(2) and 348(2).

## Medical, legal and religious advisers

**2.150**  There is a total absence of Scots case law on the admissibility of a confession to the accused's own medical adviser. In general, information given to a doctor by a patient, although confidential in the sense that the doctor has a duty not to publish it, is not regarded as being subject to legal privilege and the doctor is bound to reveal it if required to do so.[1] In *HM Advocate v Duff*[2] voluntary statements to a police casualty surgeon were admitted. However, in *Duff* the doctor was not examining the accused, his only task at that stage being to examine the dead body and certify the cause of death and as far as his relationship to the accused was concerned he was simply a private person. The admissibility of a confession to a doctor examining the accused on behalf of the police has not been the subject of express judicial decision, but in *Reid v Nixon*[3] the Crown conceded that a police doctor examining the accused for the purpose of the drink-driving legislation was 'acting as the hand of the police, and not as an independent medical referee, still less as the suspect's medical adviser'.

1 *Hume* II, 350; Alison *Practice* p 471; *Walker and Walker* p 419, § 397(c); *Wilkinson* p 105.
2 (1910) 6 Adam 248.
3 1948 JC 68.

**2.151**  In *Reid v Nixon*[1] a Full Bench laid down rules to govern the procedure for the medical examination of an accused under the drink-driving provisions and stated that the examination should take place outwith the presence of police officers and

'any interrogation of the accused by the doctor with regard to recent events should be directed solely to testing his memory and coherence and not to eliciting information bearing on his guilt, and any information bearing on his guilt which may be incidentally elicited must not be communicated to the police.'

1 1948 JC 68.

**2.152**  In one English case, *R v McDonald*[1] the Court of Appeal had to decide on the admissibility of a statement to a doctor on a non-medical matter. The defendant had been seen by a psychiatrist for the purpose of determining the issue of fitness to plead. The psychiatrist asked him why he had written a certain letter, to which McDonald replied that he had had to make up some reason for his behaviour. This statement was held to be admissible although it was observed that it will be rare to seek to adduce evidence of what the defendant has said to a doctor where the issue being tried is non-medical, and each case would have to be dealt with on its own circumstances.

1 [1991] Crim LR 122.

**2.153**  When it comes to legal advisers the position is also unclear. At the two extremes the law appears to be settled – thus a statement to the accused's legal adviser in the course of seeking his advice or instructing him is privileged and the latter is neither entitled nor bound to disclose its contents without the accused's consent[1] and at the other extreme no privilege attaches to communications made in furtherance of a criminal purpose, as where the accused seeks advice for the purpose of committing a crime.[2] It is also a clear rule that privilege flies off if the accused calls the solicitor as a witness.[3]

1 *Hume* II, 350; Alison *Practice* p 468; *Walker and Walker* p 414, § 393; *Wilkinson* p 94 ff.
2 *Dickson* p 921, § 1678 and authorities cited above.
3 1975 Act, ss 138(4) and 341(4).

**2.154** However, there is a substantial grey area and the position is unclear where the statement is made in contemplation of the solicitor–client relationship as, for example, where the accused gives certain information to a solicitor who then declines to act for him. In this case it is thought likely that the Scottish courts would follow the English view that such a communication does attract privilege.[1] Another possible problem could arise where the statement was essentially a gratuitous remark, made outwith the context of seeking advice. Professor Robert Black has expressed the tentative view that the test of whether privilege applies is the accused's purpose in disclosing the information to the solicitor. Did he do so with a view to getting professional advice? If he did not, then the statement is not protected from disclosure in legal proceedings irrespective of whether the relationship of solicitor and client existed, or still existed, or was contemplated at the time.

1 *Minter v Priest* [1930] AC 558; R Black 'A Question of Confidence' (1982) 27 JLSS 299 and 389; *Wilkinson* p 96; *Cross on Evidence* pp 389–390.

**2.155** The position regarding confessions or admissions to clergymen is similarly unclear, such authority as there is coming from an age when religion played a much greater part in life than it does today. In one old case,[1] which appears to be the only reported example, a clergyman was allowed to give parole evidence of a confession to incest which the female pannel had emitted before a Kirk Session, but this is clearly a different situation from a private confession to the clergyman.

1 *William and Isobel Cuthbert* (1842) 1 Broun 311.

**2.156** *Hume*'s view was that a private confession to a clergyman should only be excluded when made by the pannel in prison, preparing for his trial and in need of spiritual consolation.[1] Such a communication was, in his view, a separate and later incident, and no part of the story of the pannel's guilt. However, *Hume* figured the example of a man who attempts unsuccessfully to poison his wife and then being himself in poor health unburdens his conscience to a clergyman. Thereafter, having recovered his health, he resumes his attempts to kill the woman and this time is successful. *Hume* argues that in that situation the confession is 'the history of the murder and a strong circumstance in the train of the evidence against the pannel'. Accordingly, in his view, such ought to be admissible in evidence. It was also, *Hume* considered, 'not expedient to hearten criminals in the prosecution of their crimes, or to nourish them in the hope of impunity and peace of mind, by securing the secrecy, in every event, of such communication'.

1 *Hume* II, 350. See also *Anderson and Marshall* (1728) Hume II 335. Cf *Janet Hope or Walker* (1845) 2 Broun 465.

**2.157**  *Alison*[1] disagreed with *Hume*'s view (which he may have misunderstood) and argued that all communications with clergymen, these 'most sacred of human communications', should be confidential. 'Certainly', he said, 'it would be a strange anomaly if disclosures made to an attorney about the most trivial affair relating to temporal property are inviolable, and those made to a priest, for the far higher concerns of eternal welfare enjoyed no protection'.

1 *Practice* p 471.

**2.158**  *Dickson* simply repeats what *Hume* and *Alison* wrote and concludes that the point must be considered open, adding, 'It is not likely that the Court will refuse to protect communications of this nature, unless in some extreme case, such as put by Baron Hume'.[1]

1 Pages 924–925, §§ 1684–1685.

**2.159**  The law has not really progressed beyond this point and it still cannot be regarded as settled. In one unreported single-judge decision a Roman Catholic priest was allowed to plead the privilege of the confessional, but in relation to a statement made by the dying victim, not by the accused.[1]

1 *HM Advocate v Daniels* (1960) quoted in J Beltrami *The Defender* p 197.

**2.160**  The Scottish Law Commission considered that the issue of confessions to clergymen should be left alone and any problems arising resolved by the exercise of existing judicial discretion.[1] Sheriff Macphail suggests that the issue is of little practical importance since the communication is known only to the clergyman and the person who made it 'and it is difficult to envisage circumstances in which, as a practical matter, there is any likelihood of the clergyman being asked to disclose it in the Scottish courts'. While it may be unlikely, the situation could arise if a suspect for a serious crime says to the police 'I've told Father X the whole story' and then refuses to say anything else. It could well be a matter of some consequence to find out what the suspect said to the clergyman and whether it disclosed, say, 'special knowledge'. While there is probably an argument for a special status for the confessional, in the increasingly secular modern society it is difficult to see any reason of principle for a statement to a clergyman outwith the confessional to attract any higher degree of privilege than a statement to a medical adviser.

1 *Macphail* para 18.38–18.44.

**2.161**　Finally, there is also an absence of Scottish authority on the question of a confession *induced* by a religious adviser, ie where the accused has been presuaded by the cleric to unburden himself to his gaoler or to some other third party. Historically such a confession was certainly admissible in England[1] and *Alison*[2] considered that it would be admissible in Scotland also.

1 H H Joy *On the Admissibility of Confessions etc* p 49.
2 *Practice* p 586.

## Miscellaneous statements

**2.162**　In the case of *William and Isobel Cuthbert*[1] to which reference has been made above,[2] a statement made to a Kirk Session was admitted although it came as the result of questioning. This case can be regarded as an historic curiosity and the likelihood of a modern Kirk Session questioning a woman as to the paternity of her child is so remote that it can be discounted, although a similar point could conceivably arise in connection with another religious group which exercises more control over its adherents than does the contemporary Church of Scotland.

1 (1842) 1 Broun 311.
2 Para 2.155.

**2.163**　In *Robert Emond*[1] evidence of an exclamation uttered while the accused was asleep in prison was admitted. *Macdonald*[2] doubts the propriety of doing so but concedes that if the exclamation led to the discovery of real or circumstantial evidence it might be admissible to explain the discovery of the evidence. Sheriff Macphail[3] has stated the view, with which the present writer respectfully agrees, that it is wrong in principle to admit as evidence of its truth a statement uttered when the maker is not exercising his conscious mind.

1 (1830) Bell's Notes 243.
2 Page 315.
3 *Evidence* § 20.21.

**2.164**　The admissibility of a confession or admission made by a prisoner in a letter intercepted by the prison authorities is unclear. The older Scottish authorities[1] considered such evidence to be admissible and in two old cases it was allowed.[2] However, the admissibility of such evidence was implicitly doubted in *HM Advocate v Walsh*[3] although the court did not require to decide the point. Provided the letter is written voluntarily without any trap or inducement and is not subject to privilege it is difficult to see on what basis its admissibility could be objectionable. *Hume*, whose opinion was cited in *HM Advocate v Fawcett*,[4] was quite clear that:

'. . . credit cannot well be refused to a letter from the pannel which implies a confession of his guilt, or relates or alludes to the circumstances of the fact, though the letter be found even in his own pocket, and much more if it is intercepted on the way, or have passed out of his hands, for delivery according to the address.'[5]

1 *Hume* II, 396; *Burnett* p 487; Alison *Practice* p 611.
2 *Main and Atchieson* (1818) Hume II 396; *HM Advocate v Fawcett* (1869) 1 Coup 183.
3 1922 JC 82.
4 Above.
5 *Hume* II, 396.

**2.165**   In one English case the accused, while he was still at liberty shortly after the crime, wrote a letter to his wife containing highly incriminating admissions and entrusted it to a colleague for posting. The colleague intercepted it and it was passed to the police. A majority of the House of Lords upheld a decision by the Court of Appeal that the letter was admissible against the accused.[1]

1 *Rumping v DPP* [1962] 3 All ER 256. See discussion in [1962] Camb LJ 136.

**2.166**   There is no modern Scottish authority dealing with the admissibility of a statement made under the rules of a foreign jurisdiction. This issue is probably most likely to arise in connection with someone who is questioned in England under the provisions of the Police and Criminal Evidence Act 1984. PACE and its associated Codes of Practice contain minutely detailed rules designed to ensure the welfare of persons in the hands of the police which are unknown in Scotland and the PACE regime is much more stringent than Scots law. While the Scottish courts will, of course, require to look at the matter in accordance with Scots law it would seem probable that police procedures which comply with PACE will almost certainly pass the Scottish test of fairness.

# THE IMPORTANCE OF TIMEOUS OBJECTION

**2.167**   Finally, on the issue of admissibility generally, it should be pointed out that throughout this chapter it has been assumed that an objection to the admissibility of a challenged confession will be timeously intimated to the trial court. It must always be borne in mind that, whatever its source, evidence is generally admissible unless objected to[1] and it will be difficult, if not impossible, to found an appeal on the wrongful admission of a confession to which no timeous objection has been taken.

1 *Cordiner v HM Advocate* 1991 SCCR 652 at 664–665 per Lord Justice-Clerk and at 670 per Lord McCluskey. See also *Kelso v HM Advocate* 1990 SCCR 9.

# 3. Further aspects of admissibility

## IMPLIED CONFESSIONS AND ADMISSIONS

**3.01**  It has already been pointed out that silence in the face of police questioning, or when cautioned and charged, is, in general, not evidence against the accused. No inference of guilt may legitimately be drawn from the fact that the accused when charged with the crime either says nothing or says that he has nothing to say, since he is entitled to reserve his defence.

**3.02**  However, where A makes a statement in B's hearing which incriminates B and B does not disassociate himself from the statement, A's statement is relevant to support an inference that, by remaining silent, B impliedly admitted the statement. His silence in the face of accusation is tantamount to a confession. It is not correct, as is sometimes said, that A's statement is evidence against B since A's statement is hearsay and not admissible as to the truth of its contents. Rather the evidence against B is his own reaction (or lack thereof) to the statement and A's statement is only admissible for the purpose of explaining the reaction. This principle was first stated by *Dickson*[1] and appears to be generally well understood, although it has been subject to virtually no reported judicial decisions until recently.

1 *The Law of Evidence in Scotland* p 255, § 367 ff.

**3.03**  *Glover v Tudhope*[1] is an excellent example of the principle correctly applied. The accused was a transvestite who was seen talking to the drivers of two different motor vehicles. He then approached a third vehicle and spoke to the driver at which point the police approached and identified themselves to both the driver and the accused. The police had not heard the conversation themselves but the driver immediately informed them, in the hearing of the accused, that the accused had offered him 'hand relief' for £5. The accused made no response to this. After a trial at which the car driver was not called as a witness, the accused was convicted of a contravention of section 80(12) of the Criminal Justice (Scotland) Act 1980. The High Court upheld the conviction and the Lord Justice-General stated that:

'In its context what is recorded . . . is an account of the immediate reaction of the participants in the encounter between the appellant and the third motorist, and what is more important than the truth or otherwise of what the third motorist is supposed to have said, is the reaction of the appellant when it was said.'

1 1986 SCCR 49.

**3.04** Unfortunately, *Glover v Tudhope* was followed almost immediately by *Annan v Gain and Hamill*.[1] Although the decision in this case to allow the Crown appeal was justifiable on the basis of the 'special knowledge' rule, the Lord Justice-General was, with all respect, wrong in law when he asserted that where two accused made confessions in each other's presence these confessions became mutually corroborative. What ought to have been said was that where accused A made a confession in B's presence evidence of that confession was admissible in order to explain B's reaction and vice versa. In an issue concerning B, A's statement is hearsay and hence inadmissible as to the truth of its contents. Sheriff Gordon has rightly described this aspect of *Annan v Bain* as 'contrary to both principle and authority'. In *Wilson and Murray v HM Advocate* the Lord Justice-General again seemed to be tending in the same direction when he appeared to treat the similarity of separate confessions by the two accused as an adminicle of evidence.[2] However, although *Annan v Bain* has never been expressly disapproved, it is now clear, following *Buchan v HM Advocate*,[3] that if it ever represented the law it no longer does so.

1 1986 SCCR 60.
2 1987 SCCR 217 at 221–222. See further para 5.89 ff below.
3 1993 SCCR 1076 approving Renton and Brown *Criminal Procedure According to the Law of Scotland* para 18–41a.

**3.05** An implied admission can only arise if B was reasonably afforded the opportunity to repudiate A's statement.[1] On the other hand any attempt by the police to engineer the situation, for example by bringing A into B's presence solely for the purpose of having the statement made in his presence, will be liable to be held unfair.[2] *Dickson*[3] suggests that the disposition of the individual affected by the statement is a material consideration but there is no modern authority to support or contradict this view.

1 *Dickson* p 257, § 370; Walker and Walker *The Law of Evidence in Scotland* p 33, § 34.
2 *Stark and Smith v HM Advocate* 1938 JC 170; *HM Advocate v Davidson* 1968 SLT 17.
3 Page 258, § 372.

**3.06**  We have seen that following *Chalmers v HM Advocate*[1] the general law of fairness and admissibility of confessions applies to what Sheriff Macphail terms 'non-verbal assertive actions'.[2] In this area admissibility and sufficiency tend to shade into one another but it is a question of facts and circumstances in each case whether the accused's conduct can be held to amount to an admission of guilt. Thus in *Douglas v Pirie*[3] there was only a single witness to the accused's driving and it was held that the fact that the accused complied with a statutory requirement to provide a specimen of breath and did not protest that he had not been driving could not be held thereby to admit that he was driving. Similarly in *Hipson v Tudhope*[4] the accused was a passenger in a stolen car which was chased by the police and eventually crashed. In Hipson's hearing the driver told the police that the car was stolen but Hipson said nothing, only replying 'Not guilty' when cautioned and charged. There was no proof that he knew the vehicle was stolen when the journey began. The High Court drew an analogy with *Clark v HM Advocate*[5] and held that no inference of guilt could be taken from the mere silence of the accused. Thus Hipson was not to be inferred guilty of reset of the vehicle.

1  1954 JC 66; paras 1.25 and 2.45 above.
2  Macphail *Evidence* § 20.26.
3  1975 SLT 206.
4  1983 SCCR 247.
5  1965 SLT 250.

# VICARIOUS CONFESSIONS AND ADMISSIONS

**3.07**  It is a well-established rule that a statement made by one accused incriminating a co-accused and made outwith the latter's presence and hearing is not admissible against the co-accused. However, where concert is proved between two or more accused, anything said or written by any of them in relation to the preparation, execution or completion of the common enterprise is admissible against all of them: 'If acting in concert is proved, the evidence against each is, no doubt, evidence against all, *but only if concert is proved*'.[1] All the authorities emphasise the need for the proof of concert and although there is no decision directly in point it is clear that a confession of guilt after arrest by one accused would not be admissible against another since it is not made in furtherance of the common design.[2]

1  *Tobin v HM Advocate* 1934 JC 60 per Lord Justice-Clerk Aithison, emphasis added. See also *HM Advocate v Cameron* 1911 SC(J) 110; *McIntosh v HM Advocate* 1986 SCCR 496.
2  Alison *Practice* p 519; *Dickson* p 252, § 363; Macdonald *The Criminal Law of Scotland* pp 315–316; *Walker and Walker* p 35, § 37.

**3.08**  The only recent decision where a statement of this nature has been held admissible is *HM Advocate v Docherty*[1] where concert between the accused and a person now deceased was alleged. Statements by the decased incriminating the accused but made outwith his presence were held admissible. In *Jones v HM Advocate*[2] the accused was charged while acting along with another man who had pleaded guilty. Evidence of a statement by the latter implicating Jones, made outwith his presence, was agreed to be inadmissible. This point would be unlikely to arise today since statute now makes the erstwhile co-accused a competent witness for the Crown.[3]

1 1980 SLT (Notes) 33.
2 1981 SCCR 192.
3 Criminal Procedure (Scotland) Act 1975, ss 141(3) and 346(3) as amended.


## LEGAL PERSONS

**3.09**  It has been held in *Industrial Distributions (Central Scotland) Ltd v Quinn*[1] that admissions by directors of a limited company to officers of Customs and Excise who were investigating the affairs of the company were admissions by the company itself. The High Court accepted a Crown argument that the directors were the agents of the company, their admissions were to be regarded in law as the admissions of the company and a company was a legal *persona* but one which could only speak and act through the voice of an agent.

1 1984 SCCR 5.


## MIXED STATEMENTS

**3.10**  Difficult issues can arise when an accused person makes a statement containing material both incriminatory and exculpatory, the two classic examples being 'I hit him in self-defence' and 'I had sex with her but she was willing'. How much of such a statement is admissible and to what effect? The problems in arriving at an answer stem from the collision between two historical rules of Scots law, viz that admissions by the accused against his interest are generally admissible as evidence against him, and that previous exculpatory statements by an accused person are not evidence in his favour although previous statements might be admissible to show that the accused's story has been consistent.[1]

1 *Macphail* § 19.39; Wilkinson *The Scottish Law of Evidence* pp 57–59.

**3.11**  After a somewhat confused history, the law has now been settled by the seven-judge decision in *Morrison v HM Advocate*,[1] but before discussing that case it is appropriate to consider the background and the problems which have arisen. It should, of course, be remembered that the earlier texts were written when confessions to the police were largely unknown and the accused was incompetent as a witness.

1 1990 SCCR 235.

**3.12**  The problem of mixed statements is first mentioned by *Mackenzie*[1] whose view was that qualified confessions which imply a defence 'should either prove the defence or else they should not prove the libel, and either they should be altogether believed, or altogether reprobated'.

1 *Works* II, 250–251.

**3.13**  *Hume* and *Alison* both considered the issue in the context of the declaration. The former considered that the declaration should be taken with any qualification which the accused chose to make:

'Of course it cannot weigh at all against any other pannel and even as against himself, it must be taken qualified as he has chosen to give it, but liable always to be overcome in those favourable particulars, by the other evidence or presumptions in the case which often prevail against it.'[1]

Apart from the declaration, *Hume* also expressed the view that while evidence of an oral confession of guilt was admissible:

'There are obvious reasons why a pannel's denial of his guilt, or his statements in conversation afterwards of his defences against the charge, or his narrative of the way in which the thing happened cannot be admitted as evidence on his behalf.'[2]

However, he was prepared to accept that there were situations where this rule did not apply, particularly statements made at the moment when the fact libelled took place, such being part of the *res gestae* and so interwoven with the circumstances as not to be naturally separable. *Hume* commented that such statements were not liable to the same suspicion as stories told on a later occasion. He gives as an example of the practical application of the law the case of *James Wilson* where the accused's defence was that he had been constrained by fear against his will to join an armed mob. Evidence was admitted (after a debate) that he had said to a witness that he was unable to help his situation and as soon as he could he would make his escape.[3]

1 *Hume* II, 327.
2 *Hume* II, 401, note a.
3 See also *Neil Moran* (1836) Bell's Notes 285; *John Forrest* (1837) Bell's Notes 285; *Jane Pye* (1838) Bell's Notes 285.

**3.14** *Alison* took a different view and considered, in particular, that the prisoner's declaration

'. . . contains his account of the matter laid to his charge, just as the libel contains the story in regard to it told by the prosecutor. The libel may be pleaded against the prosecutor but it cannot be evidence in his favour; and in like manner the declaration may be evidence against the prisoner but cannot be founded on by him as containing proof in his favour.'[1]

This passage, and other observations by *Alison*, were later disapproved in *Morrison*.[2]

1 Alison *Practice* p 555.
2 1990 SCCR 235.

**3.15** *Dickson* does not address the question of 'mixed' statements in criminal cases, but he does consider the parallel position in civil causes, and adopts a view similar to *Hume*:

'It would be in the highest degree subversive of justice were it permissible for a party to pick out certain expressions in a conversation, or certain letters in a correspondence, and found upon them as instructing an admission by his antagonist, and not permissible for the latter to prove the whole conversation or correspondence, of which these expressions or letters form selected portions. . . . When an admission is made under a qualification, the party who founds on it must take it as it stands, and he may not adduce the portion which is favourable to him and exclude the remainder.'[1]

*Dickson*'s only observation on the evidential effect of an exculpatory statement in a declaration is brief:

'It sometimes happens that a declaration, from being probable in itself, and coinciding with other evidence, assists the case of the prisoner, in its general appearance of truthfulness leading the jury to believe his explanations of suspicious circumstances.'[2]

1 *Dickson* pp 212–213, §§ 311, 312.
2 *Dickson* p 239, § 341.

**3.16** *Macdonald*'s concise opinion was also to be criticised in *Morrison v HM Advocate*:

'Statements by the accused are not evidence in his favour. Thus an accused cannot prove letters written by herself to prove ignorance of the probable date of the birth of a child which she was accused of murdering. But where what is said is part of the *res gestae* it may be proved, as showing that the accused has throughout told a consistent story. But the facts stated are not thereby set up in his favour. It is only upon the making of the statement that he can found.'[1]

1 *Macdonald* p 316.

**3.17**   Although *Lewis*'s view was probably incorrect in strict law at the time when he wrote it (1925), it is more realistic than *Alison* or *Macdonald*, and much simpler:

'Statements made by the accused in his written declaration, when it has been duly taken before a magistrate, are admissible, and may be evidence either against the accused or in his favour, their weight and effect depending on the other evidence in the case.'[1]

1 Lewis *A Manual of the Law of Evidence in Scotland* p 314.

**3.18**   Until recently there was a surprising dearth of case law on 'mixed' statements. The first time the issue arose it did so in relation to a statement made by the accused on oath in the witness box in *Owens v HM Advocate*.[1] In this case the accused, who was charged with murder, lodged a special defence of self-defence and gave evidence in support of it, in course of which he admitted having stabbed the deceased. The Lord Justice-General observed *obiter*:

'The panel relieved the Crown of the first part of the burden [of proof] by himself admitting the stabbing with a lethal weapon, but attached to this admission the explanation of its being done in self-defence in the circumstances explained by him. The Crown cannot, we think, take advantage of the admission without displacing the explanation or at all events presenting to the jury a not less strong case that shows directly or indirectly that the explanation is false. . . . He can rely on his own sworn statement that he was acting in self-defence and rely on his own credibility to outweigh any colourable case the Crown has laid before the jury . . .'

Although *Owens* dealt solely with the issue of a 'mixed' statement given in the witness box, Sheriff Gordon has argued in his commentary to *Morrison*[2] that the decision in *Owens*, taken along with the passage from *Hume* quoted above[3] provides a possible way of dealing with 'mixed' extra-judicial statements, by saying in effect that if the Crown wishes to rely on the statement it must take it with its qualifications.

1 1946 JC 119.
2 1990 SCCR 235 at 249.
3 Para 3.13 above.

**3.19**   The first case to deal squarely with the issue of a 'mixed' extra-judicial statement was *Brown v HM Advocate*.[1] In this case the accused was charged with causing death by dangerous driving contrary to section 1 of the Road Traffic Act 1960. When the police cautioned and charged him some three weeks after the accident, he replied, 'The only thing that happened to me and the only thing I mind of is a car coming behind and going past me. I held in. My wheels caught in the soft grass. I pulled round to the other side. That is all I remember. I don't normally travel fast'. This statement was not inconsistent with the circumstances of the accident. The accused did not give evidence at the trial but, in accordance with normal practice, the Crown led evidence of the reply to caution and charge. The sheriff-substitute directed the jury that 'that explanation of the accused of itself, unless it were established really by substantive evidence is not an explanation that you would be entitled to pay any attention to'. The High Court unanimously held that this had been a misdirection and quashed the conviction. After a review of the authorities, their Lordships came to the conclusion that a statement such as had been made in the present case, having been led by the Crown, became part of the evidence in the case. It would be both unreasonable and illogical for the Crown to argue that evidence which it had led itself was not competently before the jury for consideration. The accused was entitled to found on it but only for the purpose of proving that it had been made and not as evidence of the truth of its contents.

1  1964 JC 53.

**3.20**  It seemed as it the law was firmly settled when *Brown* was approved in *Hendry v HM Advocate*[1] where the decision was clearly inspired by a growing trend by defence lawyers to use the judicial examination transcript as a substitute for evidence on oath. Hendry was charged with attempted murder. At judicial examination he gave an explanation which substantially involved self-defence but which also contained an admission of having hit the victim once or possibly twice and to having picked up a knife. The evidence was confused and confusing and the Crown put the transcript of the judicial examination in evidence. The accused did not give evidence and the trial judge directed the jury that:

'If in the course of [judicial] examination the accused makes a statement which incriminates him, then of course that would be evidence against him but . . . any statement which he makes in his favour, any exculpatory statement, is not evidence in his favour. It is only if he makes an incriminating statement that that is evidence against him.'

This approach was approved by a bench of five and the net effect of *Hendry* was that where the record of the judicial examination was put in evidence by the Crown, it became evidence against the accused, but it did not become evidence in his favour, although it might be used to establish the fact that the statement had been made or to enhance the credibility of other evidence.

1  1985 SCCR 274.

**3.21**  *Hendry* was criticised on the ground that it created distinctions which would have no meaning for jurors, one writer commenting that 'It is difficult to see how there is any distinction between making evidence more credible and being evidence itself in favour of the accused'.[1] Another point which might have been made against the decision in *Hendry* was that it was an over-reaction to a comparatively insignificant problem which might have been better dealt with by more robust use of judicial comment on the failure to give evidence on oath. Nevertheless *Hendry* had been decided by a bench of five judges including both the Lord Justice-General and the Lord Justice-Clerk, it purported to restate an historic rule of Scots law and it approved an earlier case which had stood undisturbed for over 20 years. No-one could have foreseen that within five years it was to be swept aside by a bench of seven in *Morrison*.

1  1985 SLT (News) 355.

**3.22**  The catalyst which led to *Hendry's* downfall would appear to have been the decision of the House of Lords in the English case of *R v Sharp*.[1] The specific issue in that case was whether the exculpatory parts of a statement by a defendant to a police officer constituted evidence of the truth of the facts alleged therein. *Sharp* approved the earlier decision of *R v Duncan*[2] and in particular the view of Lord Lane CJ:

'Where a "mixed" statement is under consideration by the jury in a case where the defendant has not given evidence, it seems to us the simplest, and, therefore, the method most likely to produce a just result, is for the jury to be told that the whole statement, both the incriminating parts and the excuses or explanations, must be considered by them in deciding where the truth lies. It is, to say the least, not helpful to try to explain to the jury that the exculpatory parts of the statement are something less than evidence of the facts they state. Equally, where appropriate, as it usually will be, the judge may, and should, point out that the incriminating parts are likely to be true (otherwise why say them?), whereas the excuses do not have the same weight. Nor is there any reason why, again where appropriate, the judge should not comment in relation to the exculpatory remarks upon the election of the accused not to give evidence.'

1  [1988] 1 WLR 7.
2  (1981) 73 Crim App Rep 359.

**3.23**  *Morrison* was almost the classic 'mixed' statement situation, a case of rape where the accused had admitted to the police that he had had intercourse with the victim but claimed she had been a consenting party. Evidence of his statement to the police was led by the Crown and the accused did not give evidence. The trial judge directed the jury, in accordance with *Hendry*, that a statement which was self-exonerating was not a substitute for evidence in the witness box.

**3.24** At the appeal defence counsel relied heavily on *Sharp* and eventually the Crown conceded that *Hendry* had been wrongly decided. The High Court reviewed the earlier authorities, and after disapproving certain passages from *Alison* and *Macdonald* and the decision in *Brown* in so far as it was based on *Alison*, their Lordships set out three rules to replace those in *Hendry*:

(1) As a general rule hearsay is inadmissible as evidence of the facts contained in the statement. The English definition of hearsay was accepted, viz 'an assertion other than one made by a person while giving oral evidence in the proceedings is inadmissible as evidence of any fact asserted'.[1] Their Lordships also approved *Hume's* view that a pannel's denial of guilt or his statements in conversation afterwards were inadmissible[2] and the opinion of the court in *Meehan v HM Advocate*[3] that '[I]t has never been competent for the defence to avoid the giving of evidence by the accused by leading evidence of the accused having denied his guilt extrajudicially to friends or advisers as proof of his innocence'. Accordingly an accused is not entitled to lead in evidence a prior statement, which is to any extent exculpatory, as to the truth of its contents unless the statement is truly part of the *res gestae*.

(2) Where the Crown leads in evidence, or where evidence is led by the defence without Crown objection, of a prior statement which is capable of being both incriminatory and exculpatory, the whole statement is admissible as evidence of the facts it contains, since it would be unfair to admit the admission without the explanation. The trial judge should direct the jury that it must consider the whole statement and determine whether the whole or any part of it is accepted by it as the truth.

(3) A prior statement of an accused which is not to any extent incriminatory is admissible for the limited purpose of proving that the statement was made and of the attitude or reaction of the accused at the time when it was made, but not as evidence of the facts contained in it. Such a statement is only admissible for the purpose of proving that the accused's story has been consistent. An accused could lead evidence of such a statement where he has given evidence and his story has been challenged as a late invention, but only for the purpose of rebutting the challenge to his credibility. This rule is also to apply in the situation where the Crown leads evidence of an exculpatory statement (most probably a reply to caution and charge); in this case the accused may found

on the statement but only for the purpose of showing that his story
has been consistent.

1 *Cross on Evidence* (6th edn) p 38 approved in *Sharp* [1988] 1 WLR 7 at 11.
2 *Hume* II, 401.
3 1970 JC 11.

**3.25** In *Morrison* the High Court also stated that when directing a jury
regarding a 'mixed' statement, the trial judge may well feel it desirable to
comment on the weight which the jury may wish to place on the different
parts of the statement, and particularly the fact that it was not made on
oath and was not subject to cross-examination. However, the Scottish
reluctance to comment on a failure to give evidence once again raised its
head, and although their Lordships said that they did not seek to inhibit
the right of a judge to make such a comment, it 'should be made with
restraint and only where there are special circumstances which require it'.

**3.26** *Morrison* has now settled the basic issue of the admissibility of a
'mixed' statement. Such a statement is admissible as evidence of its
contents and it is up to the jury to decide what to make of it. However,
it does leave some important points undecided, notably the question
of evidential sufficiency. Is the statement to be separable into its
component parts or is it to be treated as a single indivisible unit? If the
former approach is correct, a statement such as 'I hit him in self-
defence' would be capable of providing the Crown with corroboration
of the victim's evidence, since the jury could believe the first part ('I
hit him') and disbelieve the second ('in self-defence'). However, the
second approach, which was adopted in *Owens*,[1] is consistent with
*Hume* and enjoys the support of Sheriff Gordon.[2] Although *Owens*
was mentioned in *Morrison* it was not in the context of sufficiency. If a
mixed statement falls to be treated as a single unit, the Crown will
have to take it with its qualifications and will, at the least, have to be in
a position to, in *Hume's* words, 'overcome [it] in those favourable particulars by the other evidence or presumptions in the case'.

1 1946 JC 119.
2 1990 SCCR 235 at 249.

**3.27** Since *Morrison* was decided, the 'single unit' approach has
received further support in the case of *Higgins v HM Advocate*[1] in
which the High Court quoted with apparent approval the statement in
*Owens* that 'The Crown cannot, we think, take advantage of the
admission without displacing the explanation or at all events
presenting to the jury a not less strong case that shows directly or
indirectly that the explanation is false'.

1 1993 SCCR 542.

**3.28** Another unresolved issue in *Morrison* is a suggestion that different rules may apply in the case of statements made at judicial examination. It is respectfully submitted that there is no basis in principle for such a distinction and the observation in *Morrison* is little more than a hint. However, the point remains open. The briefly-reported case of *Howarth v HM Advocate*[1] has indicated that the High Court is of the view that *exculpatory* statements at judicial examination can only be founded on by an accused if he gives evidence at his trial and even then the statement is only admissible to show consistency. On the basis of *Howarth*, statements at judicial examination do not form an exception to the rule against hearsay.

1 1992 GWD 10–523.

**3.29** *Morrison* is a difficult case and is always going to remain so. It was applied, 'retrospectively' as it were, in *Jones and Collins v HM Advocate*[1] where the trial judge had directed the jury on the basis of *Hendry* shortly before that case was overruled by *Morrison*. The Crown conceded that there had been a misdirection. One odd feature of *Jones and Collins* is that Jones himself had actually given evidence and the Lord Justice-Clerk pointed out that the direction complained of had thus no application to him. It is therefore difficult to understand why the court then went on to hold that there had been a miscarriage of justice in relation to Jones, although as Sheriff Gordon points out the decision can be justified on the ratio that the judge's charge as a whole was confusing in its terms.

1 1991 SCCR 290.

**3.30** Some of the problems arising from *Morrison* and which will undoubtedly recur, were seen in *Khan v HM Advocate*[1] where one of the two main issues for the appeal court concerned the test to be applied in determining whether a statement can be held to be truly 'mixed', (ie partly incriminatory and partly exculpatory) or wholly exculpatory. The point is of considerable importance in deciding whether the judge requires to direct the jury in the terms of rule 2 or rule 3 in *Morrison*. *Khan* makes it clear that if the statement is led by the Crown, who rely on it as being at least partly incriminatory, rule 2 is applicable and it does not matter whether there is other evidence pointing to the truth of the admissions. This is relatively straightforward. For the purpose of rule 2 the test of whether the statement is part incriminatory is whether a reasonable jury would be entitled so to regard it in the knowledge of all the facts about the case.

1 1992 SCCR 146.

**3.31** Much more difficult is the second question – what happens if a partly-incriminatory statement is led by the defence, without Crown objection, for entirely self-serving purposes? In this situation is the judge required to direct the jury in terms of rule 2 or rule 3? If the former applies, there is a danger that the defence could get the accused's version before the jury without his giving evidence, one of the motivating factors behind the now discredited decision in *Hendry*.

**3.32** In *Khan* the High Court rather fudged this issue. While it almost held that the trial judge, who had followed rule 3, had misdirected the jury it did not actually do so. Instead it held that regard had to be had to the use of the statement made at the trial and it would be an abuse of rule 2 to apply it in circumstances where there could be no unfairness to the accused. In the circumstances of *Khan* it was held that the judge was correct to direct the jury on the basis of rule 3. At the time when the statement was led in evidence, the Crown could not have objected since it was unknown whether the accused was to give evidence and it could well have been the intention of the defence to use it to show consistency of his account. In this situation the High Court clearly felt it would have been unreasonable to allow the defence to take advantage of rule 2 and effectively to have its cake and eat it.

**3.33** While this decision is, with respect, sensible and pragmatic, it is nevertheless a departure from rule 2 in *Morrison* which made no reference to the use made of the statement. It would seem that rule 2 is now to be read as saying that a mixed statement is admissible as evidence of the facts that it contains when it is led by the Crown or by the defence without Crown objection but only *if it was competent for the Crown to object*. Otherwise rule 3 will apply.

**3.34** In *Scaife v HM Advocate*[1] the High Court reiterated that where evidence of a mixed extra-judicial statement is led by the Crown it is admissible as evidence of the facts contained in it. Even if the accused does not give evidence the trial judge must nevertheless direct the jury that it must determine whether the whole or any part of the statement is accepted by it as the truth. The jury also require to be directed that if it believes the exculpatory part of the accused's statement or it raises a reasonable doubt in its mind it should acquit him.

1 1992 SCCR 845.

## CONFIRMATION BY SUBSEQUENT FACT

**3.35** It may happen that in the course of making a confession which is later held to be inadmissible, an accused brings to light evidence which is relevant to the case and which the prosecution wishes to tender. For example, he might say during the course of a confession that he threw the murder weapon into a particular field or that stolen property is in his house and the object is searched for and found. It may, of course, be that the object has some evidential value independent of the confession, for example the accused's fingerprints might be found on the weapon or the stolen property might be in a locked room for which only the accused holds the key. However, where the confession is inadmissible two basic questions arise: (1) how is the law to treat such evidence when it is discovered as a consequence of an inadmissible confession? and (2) should the confession or some part of it also be admitted if it is verified by the subsequently discovered evidence?

**3.36** There is little Scottish authority on these questions, particularly the former, but in England, prior to the passing of the Police and Criminal Evidence Act 1984, the situation was precisely the opposite with an excess of authorities, many of which were mutually contradictory. On the basis of English authority there are five possible answers to the two questions: (a) to admit the fact discovered but nothing more; (b) to admit the fact discovered, and that its discovery was in consequence of something the accused said; (c) to admit the fact discovered together with as much of the confession as relates strictly to it; (d) to admit the fact discovered and the entire confession; and (e) to exclude the whole confession and all facts discovered in consequence of it.[1]

1 A Gottlieb 'Confirmation by Subsequent Facts' (1956) 72 LQR 209; *Macphail* § 21.02.

**3.37** Alison[1] favoured answer (a) which derived from the old case of *R v Warickshall*.[2] In *Warickshall* a female prisoner, in the course of an improperly induced confession, said that the stolen goods were in her lodgings. A subsequent search revealed that this was indeed so, and the goods were actually found in her bedding. Although the confession was excluded, the fact of the finding of the stolen goods was admitted. This is the position to which section 76(4) of PACE has now returned English law. On the other hand, *Dickson*[3] regarded answer (b) as 'both just and discriminating' although the only comparable Scottish authority at that time[4] is most appropriately viewed as an example of answer (e).

1 II p 584.
2 1 Leach CC 263; See also H H Joy *On the Admissibility of Confessions etc* pp 81–88.
3 Page 244, § 350.
4 *Ann Watt or Ketchen* (1834) Bell's Notes 244.

**3.38**  Since *Dickson*'s time the only reported decision bearing on the point is *Chalmers v HM Advocate*[1] and it is less than ideally clear, particularly in relation to the evidential value of evidence discovered as the result of an inadmissible confession.[2] It will be remembered that following an interrogation, subsequently found to have been unfair, Chalmers had taken the police to a cornfield where he pointed out where he had disposed of the deceased's purse, which was duly recovered. The evidence of the accused's actings in the cornfield was admitted by the trial judge, in the absence of authority to the contrary. However, his decision was overturned on appeal. Lord Cooper dealt with the 'episode of the cornfield' simply on the basis that the crucial evidential point was the accused's knowledge of the whereabouts of the purse:

'The significance of the episode is plain, for it showed that the appellant knew where the purse was. If the police had simply produced, and proved the finding of, the purse, that evidence would have carried them little or no distance in his case towards implicating the appellant.'

Since the accused's actings in the field were 'part and parcel of the same transaction' as the unfair interrogation, evidence of them was inadmissible and there was accordingly nothing to link the accused to the purse. The finding of the purse on its own was irrelevant and hence the case collapsed.

1 1954 JC 66.
2 See Cowen and Carter *Essays on the Law of Evidence* pp 41–71.

**3.39**  Two basic propositions can be derived from *Chalmers*. Firstly, although the point was not specifically argued, the discovery of a subsequent fact does not, in Scots law, render an otherwise inadmissible confession admissible. This much at least is clear. Secondly, and more doubtfully, it would appear that the evidence of the finding of the purse would have been admissible *quantum valeat* (which in this case was, of course, nil). At the very least Lord Cooper was not prepared in the circumstances of *Chalmers* to hold that the finding was inadmissible. However, the point certainly cannot be regarded as being beyond doubt.

**3.40**  Given that Scots law is unsettled on the issue of the admissibility of a fact discovered in consequence of an inadmissible confession, it is appropriate to consider the arguments that might be advanced. One of the main reasons for the unsatisfactory state of the pre-PACE law in England was the failure of the courts to decide the policy behind the exclusion of improperly obtained confessions. This is not so much of an issue in Scotland since the sole criterion is fairness to the accused, and improperly obtained evidence will be excluded because it has been improperly obtained and not because it is unreliable. Similarly, there are relatively few instances in Scots law of the courts expressly excluding evidence in order to discourage improper police practices. However, even though the courts may not overtly apply the disciplinary principle, the fact that a case has collapsed because improperly obtained evidence has been excluded is bound to become known to the police and it is reasonable to assume that lessons will be learned. In other words the exclusion of evidence will be likely to have an effect on police behaviour whatever the court's intention may be.

**3.41** Accordingly, it might be argued that the need to discourage improper police actions must lead to the conclusion that where the confession is inadmissible, evidence of a consequently discovered fact ought also to be inadmissible. The exclusion of an improperly obtained confession in order to discourage improper police behaviour is inconsistent with the admission of evidence discovered in consequence of the confession. However, the superficially attractive argument ignores the fact that the existence of the evidence is a matter independent of the confession. Let us suppose that, in the course of an inadmissible confession, A admits to having pawned the stolen property in the shop run by B. B is seen by the police, remembers A pawning the property, which is recovered, and in due course he is cited as a witness against A. An argument that the prosecution should not be allowed to call B as a witness against A because his involvement was discovered as the result of an inadmissible confession is self-evidently unsustainable, even if it were a practical proposition for the defence to get the point before the court.[1] In the hypothetical example, B's evidence linking A with the property would clearly be admissible and since B is merely a link in the chain of evidence between A and the property, there is, it is submitted, no difference in principle between the hypothetical example and the situation where the inadmissible confession leads simply to the discovery of the property itself without B's intervention, the link to A being provided by, say, fingerprints.

1 See *R v Lockhart* (1785) 1 Leach CC 386.

**3.42** On the other hand, if unreliability is considered to be the reason for the exclusion of an improperly obtained confession, an argument can be made that while there may be a risk that the confession is un-reliable, no such risk attaches to the subsequently discovered fact. It has already been pointed out that this is not the basis on which Scots law operates, but such an argument would tend towards the conclusion that at least so much of the confession as is verified (and hence proved reliable) by the finding of the fact should be admitted.

**3.43** The Thomson Committee dealt with the issue briefly under reference to *Chalmers*:

'The view that the discovery of the article renders any part of the statement admissible has been rejected in Scotland. We accept this. Scots law excludes evidence on the ground that it has been improperly obtained without consideration of its reliability. To allow evidence of a statement to be led because it can be shown to be true might encourage police irregularity. On the other hand, it does not follow that evidence of the discovery of articles should be excluded merely because the information supplied by an accused which led to their discovery, is inadmissible. We take the view that there is nothing impro-per in the police asking questions of an accused person after charge, for example regarding the whereabouts of a missing child or stolen property. Indeed the police have a duty to ask such questions and the public expect them to do so. Although the answers which they receive will not be admissible in evidence, the court may allow evidence of recovery, provided (a) the pros-ecution does not disclose in evidence the source of the information; and (b) the information was not obtained by methods which the court decides are unfair.'[1]

1 Departmental Committee on Criminal Procedure in Scotland (Second Report) (1975, Cmnd 6218) paras 7.26 and 7.27.

**3.44** Unless the Thomson Committee was intending to restrict the admissibility of recovery solely to the post-charge questioning situation, the difficulty with this approach is that it is circular. Apart from post-charge questioning, where any resulting statement is inadmissible no matter how 'fair' the questioning, it is illogical to say that the evidence is admissible unless it was obtained by methods which were unfair, since the only basis on which Scots law now excludes confessions is that they were unfairly obtained. On this approach, if the confession is excluded because it has been unfairly obtained, *ex hypothesi* the subsequent fact is also inadmissible. This is clearly not in accordance with Lord Cooper's opinion in *Chalmers* nor, it is submitted, is it consistent with logic.

**3.45** It is remarkable that there is so little authority on this point in Scotland and it is not possible to draw any firm conclusions as to how the courts will treat future cases of this nature. However it is submitted, with respect, that the most appropriate solution to the problem of confirmation by subsequent fact is suggested by Sheriff Macphail who has argued that the issue should be assimilated to the broader question of illegal searches and seizures, with the issue becoming one of judicial discretion:

'If the facts were discovered as a result of circumstances particularly unfair to the accused or an exceptionally serious illegality, such as a confession extracted by brutality, the judge would be entitled to exclude the evidence. That would then be a particular application of the general discretion of the court to admit or exclude evidence illegally or irregularly obtained.'[1]

1 *Macphail* § 21.04.

# 4. Procedural aspects

## INTRODUCTION

**4.01** Historically, the decision whether a confession was admissible was regarded as a matter of law for the judge. In practical terms, what would happen was that the Crown would lead evidence up to the point when the statement was about to be tendered, the defence would then object, the jury would be excluded and the judge would hear legal arguments in their absence. If the judge was able to decide the point on the basis of the legal submissions he would do so. However if, as happened in *Chalmers v HM Advocate*,[1] the judge felt unable to give a proper ruling without hearing evidence, the jury would be brought back and the evidence would be taken in its presence. Thereafter the judge would rule whether the statement was admissible or not. This procedure created two problems. Firstly, the legal argument might have to be based on disputed hypotheses as to what witnesses might say, which was clearly unsatisfactory. Secondly, although the procedure was consistent with the rule that all the evidence had to be taken in the presence of the jury,[2] it did mean that if the judge decided that the statement was inadmissible, the jury would require to be directed to disregard evidence which it had heard. According to Lord Thomson in *Chalmers*, 'Experience shows that if the jury is present some prejudice to the accused is likely to occur'.

1 1954 JC 66.
2 Act 1587 c57. See Macphail *Evidence* § 20.38.

## CHALMERS V HM ADVOCATE AND THE TRIAL WITHIN A TRIAL

**4.02** The High Court produced a major innovation in Scottish procedure when Lord Justice-General Cooper and Lord Justice-Clerk Thomson took the opportunity presented by *Chalmers*[1] to lay down the trial within a trial procedure:

'When objection is taken to a line of evidence based upon the alleged unfairness of the methods used in eliciting it, the jury ought to be excluded, and the evidence bearing upon the attendant circumstances should be heard by the judge in the absence of the jury, including if so advised the evidence of the accused himself. If, in the light of such evidence and argument, the judge sustains the objection, the jury should be told nothing about the matter. If on the other hand the judge repels the objection, the case will proceed in the presence and hearing of the jury, and, if either prosecution or defence choose to do so, the evidence bearing upon the attendant circumstances, can be made the subject of examination and cross-examination a second time. In the end of the day it will be for the judge to direct the jury that, in considering the weight and value of the evidence to which objection has been taken and repelled, it is for the jury to have regard to the attendant circumstances as proved before them, and, in so far as they may consider that the evidence objected to is not to be relied upon by reason of the circumstances in which it arose, to discount it or exclude it from their deliberations.'

Lord Cooper recognised that the procedure 'may give rise to difficulty and may not always achieve the desired ideal of avoiding prejudice to the accused. But it will at least minimise the risk of such prejudice to an extent unattainable by our past practice'. Thus the purpose of the trial within a trial procedure is to exclude from the knowledge of the jury an item of evidence which turns out to be inadmissible, but the admissibility of which cannot be determined without the court knowing about the attendant circumstances. The theoretical benefit of the procedure is that it ensures that before a jury hears the disputed evidence, the judge has satisfied himself that the admissibility cannot be determined except on consideration of the issue of credibility, which is a matter for the jury.

1 1954 JC 66 at 80 and 82.

**4.03** It is unclear, and in any event of little importance, whether the High Court intended to assimilate Scottish practice to the well-established *voire dire* procedure in England. However, compared to the English procedure the Scottish trial within a trial has remained largely undeveloped. When regard is had to the complex and occasionally curious body of case law which grew up around the English procedure, especially before PACE, that may be no bad thing.[1] The judges in *Chalmers* gave no assistance as to how the Scottish courts were to approach anything other than the most basic issues involved and no guidance has been offered then or subsequently on issues such as the burden and standard of proof which have caused acute difficulties in the common law countries.[2] The only time such matters appear to have arisen in Scotland they did so inconclusively in *McGungle v HM Advocate*.[3]

1 Eg P Mirfield *Confessions* pp 93–102.
2 See *Cross on Evidence* (7th edn) pp 171–172.
3 1990 SCCR 320; para 4.12 below.

## THE DECLINE OF THE TRIAL WITHIN A TRIAL

**4.04**   Criticism of the trial within a trial first appeared in *Thompson v HM Advocate*[1] where, following a trial within a trial, the trial judge had admitted a disputed confession but in doing so had suggested that the time had come for the views expressed in *Chalmers* to be reconsidered. In the appeal court, Lord Justice-General Clyde endorsed the trial judge's observation:

'Experience has shown that [the trial within a trial] has several undesirable features. Apart from the repetition of evidence (first before the judge alone, and then before the jury) with the consequent addition to the length of time occupied by the trial, it affords an opportunity for the reconstruction of evidence for the second trial after the witnesses have seen how they are cross-examined in the first one. Moreover the jury in the second trial have no opportunity of testing the consistency of the evidence in the two trials, because they are not present at the first one, whereas the judge is, although he cannot properly disclose the inconsistencies to the jury. It seems unfair to both sides that the judge should be put in a stronger position than the jury to decide on a matter where ultimate responsibility for deciding rests exclusively with the jury. . . . If the question is whether the confession has been freely and voluntarily given – and that is usually the question – and if, as seems clear, the jury must have an opportunity of determining whether the confession was fairly obtained, in cases where the confession is part of the Crown evidence in the trial, it seems difficult to justify a separate trial on this matter before the judge alone as well. It would seem that there is much to be said for leading the evidence once and for all before the jury. If the judge takes the view that the Crown has not led evidence that the confession was freely and voluntarily given, he can at the end of the day direct the jury to disregard the evidence of the confession . . . But if he considers that the confession was freely and voluntarily given, then he leaves the matter to the jury. Time would be saved and the interests of the accused would be quite adequately safeguarded in this way.'

1  1968 JC 61.

**4.05**   In *Murphy v HM Advocate*[1] the trial judge had held a trial within a trial but, with considerable hesitation, allowed the disputed confession to go to the jury. The appeal court upheld him, the leading judgment being given by Lord Wheatley who had by now become Lord Justice-Clerk. His Lordship stressed the bilateral element which was now regarded as inherent in the question of fairness and he offered some guidance on the test to be applied at the trial within a trial:

'(1) If an issue turns on credibility it is for the jury to decide that issue and not the judge; (2) If two possible interpretations can properly be put on the situation, one of which falls into the category of fairness and the other into the category of unfairness, the judge should leave the determination of that issue to the jury.'

1 1975 SLT (Notes) 17.

**4.06** In *Balloch v HM Advocate*[1] Lord Wheatley added to his earlier comments on the relative positions of judge and jury:

'Suffice it to say, a Judge who has heard the evidence regarding the manner in which a challenged statement was made will normally be justified in withholding the evidence from the jury only if he is satisfied on the undisputed relevant evidence that no reasonable jury could hold that the statement had been voluntarily made and had not been extracted by unfair or improper means. Applying that test to the instant case, we are of the opinion that, to say the least, the question was so open that the trial Judge acted perfectly correctly in allowing the issue to go to the jury for their determination.'

1 1977 JC 23.

**4.07** The procedure suggested by *Thompson* and *Balloch* requires implicit faith in the ability of juries to assess properly the issue of fairness and then, if finding the confession unfairly obtained, to put it out of their minds completely. In the absence of properly conducted research, opinions for or against the capability of juries to discharge this task must necessarily rest on little more than anecdote and personal opinion. Witnesses who appeared before the Thomson Committee suggested that 'Commonsense and experience indicate that it is fallacious to think that a jury can completely ignore inadmissible evidence which they have heard, no matter how much they are told to do so'.[1] Counsel for Balloch had touched on this point when he argued that a judge should be reluctant to let such an issue go to the jury because the question of the fairness of the eliciting of a statement is not readily understood by a jury. Lord Wheatley dismissed this as a 'somewhat startling' proposition, which '. . . not only flies in the face of the test which the Judge has to apply in deciding whether the evidence should be admitted to or excluded from the jury, but would appear to desiderate that the Judge should usurp the function of the jury in what *ex hypothesi* has become a question of fact'.

1 Departmental Committee on Criminal Procedure in Scotland (Second Report) (1975, Cmnd 6218) para 47.06.

**4.08** The same point was made in an article in the Scots Law Times,[1] the writer of which criticised *Balloch*, and the whole trend of the decisions leading up to it, on the basis that the jury was being asked, in effect, to regard as 'unfair' the confession and consequent conviction of an accused whom *ex hypothesi* it regards as guilty. The writer questioned whether the judge's function as defined in *Balloch* left any room for the trial within a trial at all and suggested that the High Court should reconsider *Chalmers* and move unequivocally in one direction or the other, something which has yet to happen.

1 1977 SLT 140.

**4.09** English commentators, used to the *voire dire*, find the *Balloch* approach difficult to understand. Thus, Peter Mirfield describes Lord Wheatley's view that fairness was '*ex hypothesi* a question of fact' as 'puzzling'.[1] The English would regard such a question as encompassing questions of law as well as fact. Mirfield draws a distinction between the issue of what was said and done, an issue of pure fact, and the issue of whether what one decides was said and done amounts to unfair treatment of the accused, an issue involving the application of law to facts. It follows, he says, that either the judge must decide the facts and apply the law to them (the English and *Chalmers* approach) or the jury must do this and, while there may be reasons for adopting the latter method, it is unhelpful to castigate the former as usurping the function of the jury. Like the Thomson Committee's witnesses and the anonymous Scots Law Times' contributor, Mirfield considers that Lord Wheatley's approach gives insufficient weight to the difficulty which juries might have in excluding from their minds evidence which they have decided is inadmissible and he adds that juries would be likely to be tempted to use the evidence anyway without coming to any decision on the question of admissibility.

1 *Confessions* p 201.

**4.10** Despite these criticisms, *Balloch* has remained the definitive statement of Scots law on the entitlement of a trial judge to withdraw a disputed confession from the jury. The 'no reasonable jury' test has been reiterated on many occasions, notably *Lord Advocate's Reference (No 1 of 1983)*[1] and *Montes v HM Advocate*.[2] Such further comments as the High Court has made on the trial within a trial have been uniformly critical. In *Hartley v HM Advocate*[3] it was described as a 'lamentable process, so often now condemned'. In *HM Advocate v Whitelaw*[4] Lord Cameron repelled an objection to the admissibility of a statement and refused to hold a trial within a trial, commenting that:

'Evidence as to statements of a possibly incriminating character alleged to have been made by an accused person is prima facie of the highest relevance and the jury's function should not be in fact usurped unless it is abundantly clear that the rules of fairness and fair dealing have been flagrantly transgressed and it would be better for a jury seized of the whole evidence in the case and of all the circumstances, under such guidance as they should receive from the presiding judge, themselves to take that decision as to the extent to which, if at all, they will take into account evidence of statements . . . given by a suspect after due caution.'

This observation was later approved by the appeal court in *Tonge v HM Advocate*.[5] Lord Cameron again refused a trial within a trial in *HM Advocate v Gilgannon*[6] although on this occasion he ruled the statement inadmissible. In *HM Advocate v Mair*[7] Lord Hunter considered that the trial within a trial had 'a number of unsatisfactory and rather dangerous features and may conflict with the normal practice in our criminal procedure that the whole evidence should be led in the presence of the jury' and it 'should only be used sparingly and in very special circumstances'.

1 1984 SCCR 62.
2 1990 SCCR 645.
3 1979 SLT 26.
4 1980 SLT (Notes) 25.
5 1982 JC 130.
6 1983 SCCR 10.
7 1982 SLT (Notes) 471.

## THE TRIAL WITHIN A TRIAL – THE PRESENT POSITION

**4.11** Despite the repeated criticism to which it has subjected the trial within a trial, so far the High Court has not fully reconsidered *Chalmers*, and the trial within a trial is not yet a spent force. A few recent examples may be found where it has been used by the trial court without any apparent criticism from the appeal court.[1] Nevertheless, the 'no reasonable jury' test means that there will be few situations in which the trial within a trial will result in evidence being withheld from the jury. Before the judge is obliged (or possibly entitled) to withhold a confession from the jury there must be no conflict of evidence as to the circumstances in which the statement was made and it must be abundantly clear on the undisputed evidence that it was unfairly obtained. This is a very stringent test. It is for the jury, and not the judge, to decide on credibility and if the situation can be interpreted as either fair or unfair, the interpretation is also for the jury. It has been said that 'The statement must go to the jury if the account of the circumstances spoken to by any one witness indicates that it may not have been taken unfairly'.[2] On this basis there would appear to be much force in the criticism that the procedure will only serve to lengthen the trial without any advantage to the administration of justice.[3]

1  Eg *Aiton v HM Advocate* 1987 SCCR 252; *McGungle v HM Advocate* 1990 SCCR 320.
2  Renton and Brown *Criminal Procedure According to the Law of Scotland* para 18–42.
3  *Macphail* § 20.47.

**4.12**  Recently some consideration has been given to the interpretation of the phrase 'undisputed relevant evidence'. In *McGungle v HM Advocate*[1] two of the accused had given incriminatory statements some 12 hours after caution and charge. It was alleged that these statements had been made following threats and physical violence by plain-clothed police officers. Sheriff Risk held a trial within a trial 'to discover if there was any undisputed basis of fact' for a decision on admissibility. Two of the accused gave evidence in their own right and made detailed allegations of police malpractice and this was, to an extent, supported by one of their co-accused who was called as a witness. The Crown led evidence from a single police officer who had taken the statements and who stated that he had done nothing improper and had seen no sign of injury on the accused. No evidence was led from any of the officers who were alleged to have behaved improperly. The defence argued that the onus was on the Crown to demonstrate that the statements had been fairly obtained. Since the Crown had provided no explanation and led no evidence to contradict the accused's version, on the 'uncontested evidence' the statements were inadmissible. The Crown, on the other hand, argued that since the issue of unfairness depended on credibility it should be left to the jury.

1  1990 SCCR 320.

**4.13**  The sheriff allowed the statements to go to the jury and in his subsequent report to the High Court he offered the following observations on what 'undisputed relevant evidence' meant:

'The solicitors for the appellants argued that the evidence of unfairness in this case was "undisputed" because the Crown had been unable to adduce any witness to contradict what was said by [the accused and the co-accused]. I do not think that this is the situation envisaged by Lord Wheatley when he used the expression "undisputed relevant evidence". It seems to me that he was referring to a situation in which parties can argue the admissibility of a statement from an undisputed basis of fact. In the present case the allegations made by the accused were sharply challenged by the Crown in cross-examination; to my mind that places their evidence in dispute. That being so I felt obliged to allow the jury to resolve the dispute.'

Unfortunately a potentially interesting appeal fizzled out because the Crown conceded that the statements should not have been allowed to go to the jury. Nevertheless, the High Court did not criticise the sheriff's definition of 'undisputed' and it would appear that in this context it should be read as meaning 'agreed' rather than 'uncontradicted'.

**4.14** When, then, should the trial court hold a trial within a trial? The High Court has given little guidance as to the criteria which the trial judge should apply when considering the issue. Probably the clearest statement came from Lord Cameron in *HM Advocate v Whitelaw*:

'I have never been in favour of any extention of the practice of a trial within a trial unless . . . the circumstances already established or admitted are such as to be prima facie indicative of unfairness towards an accused who is in the hands of the police and of fundamental rules of fairness which lie at the root of our criminal procedure.'[1]

1 1980 SLT (Notes) 25 at 26.

**4.15** Clearly, if there is no dispute as to the facts, a trial within a trial is superfluous. In this case the trial judge may (and possibly should) decide the issue of admissibility without one as was done in *HM Advocate v Whitelaw*, *HM Advocate v Gilgannon* and *HM Advocate v Mair*.[1] However, if Sheriff Risk's interpretation of 'undisputed relevant evidence' is correct, and the High Court took no issue with it, it would appear that even where there is a dispute as to the facts, there is little scope for the trial within a trial. If the Crown and defence agree the facts the judge can deal with the point. If they don't, there is, almost *ipso facto*, no 'undisputed relevant evidence' and the issue becomes one for the jury. Lord Cameron's observation above would tend to suggest that a trial within a trial should only be held if the court is 'teetering on the brink' of holding a statement inadmissible and, presumably, the Crown declines to concede the point.[2]

1 Para 4.10 above.
2 See also *Renton and Brown* para 18–44.

**4.16** Against this background it may reasonably be asked whether the continuing retention of the trial within a trial serves any useful purpose or whether it would be better simply to dispense with it. The strongest argument in favour of the trial within a trial appears to be that it avoids the jury hearing evidence which it is then directed to disregard. This is one of the main reasons why English law adheres so strongly to the concept of the *voire dire*. However, Scots law appears to have a higher degree of faith in the ability of its juries and it is submitted that the abolition of the trial within a trial would make little practical difference to the present position. In 1975 the Thomson Committee noted that 'The procedure has been in existence now for some twenty years and the number of cases in which it has resulted in evidence being excluded is very few indeed.' There seems no reason to think that the position has altered materially during the succeeding years.

## SOLEMN PROCEDURE – OTHER ISSUES

**4.17**   In *Boyne v HM Advocate*[1] the 16-year-old accused had been questioned at some length by the police and certain admissions had been made. At the trial no objection was taken to the evidence of the police questioning and although he gave evidence the accused said nothing about unfairness or anything done by the police having influenced him. The trial judge directed the jury that there was no evidence before it from which it could hold that the statements had been unfairly obtained, although he was careful to point out that it could have regard to all the circumstances when assessing the quality of the evidence. On appeal the High Court considered that on this aspect there was nothing objectionable in the judge's charge. It added its own observations on the failure to give evidence on the question of unfairness:

'The points taken by [defence counsel] to support his claim for unfairness were founded not on any direct evidence but on inferences to be drawn from the youth of the appellant . . . the length of the questioning and the hours at which the questioning took place. There was, however, no evidence, and least of all from the appellant, that these factors had any effect on him in giving the statements or influenced him in any way. . . . [T]he judge was entitled to hold that there was no evidence on which a reasonable jury could find that the statements had been extracted unfairly from Boyne in the legal sense.'

The High Court did not, of course, say that the accused is required to give evidence expressly on the question of unfairness (or even give evidence at all) before the jury would be entitled to hold a confession to have been unfairly obtained. Howver, it is clear that before it may do so there must be actual evidence of unfairness. Counsel's theories and inferences are not good enough.

1 1980 JC 47.

**4.18**   A most interesting question was raised, but unfortunately not resolved, in *McGee v HM Advocate*.[1] The accused had been interviewed on tape and at his trial objection was taken to the admissibility of the taped interview and its transcript on the grounds of unfairness. Having heard the parties the trial judge upheld the objection on the view that the accused had been subjected to 'systematic questioning which amounted to cross-examination'. However, defence counsel then proceeded to cross-examine one of the interviewing officers in relation to information given to him by the accused in the course of the interview. The Crown argued that it would be contrary to the interests of justice to allow only selected excerpts of the interview to go to the jury and that by, in effect, seeking to lead part of the accused's statement, the defence must be held to have waived the objection previously taken. The trial judge upheld this submission and, notwithstanding his earlier ruling, allowed the whole interview to be put in evidence, leaving it to the jury to decide at the end of the day whether the statement had resulted from unfair interrogation. When the matter came before the appeal court, defence counsel intimated that he was no longer proposing to argue this issue and the appeal court was deprived of the opportunity of pronouncing on the issue.

1 1990 SCCR 710.

**4.19** In one highly unusual case, *Styr v HM Advocate*[1] the defence invoked the preliminary diet procedure under section 76 of the Criminal Procedure (Scotland) Act 1975 in order to seek a ruling *inter alia* on the admissibility of tape-recorded statements made by the accused to inspectors appointed under section 177 of the Financial Services Act 1986. Although opposed by the Crown, the sheriff held that where a statement had been reduced to a transcript he was entitled to consider its admissibility at a preliminary diet. In the event he decided to let the matter go to the jury. It is unfortunate that the novel procedural point passed apparently unnoticed in the High Court but this does seem to be an extension of the preliminary diet into altogether new territory.

1 1993 SCCR 278. See D B Griffiths 'Interviews with Suspects, Two Unusual Cases' Greens Criminal Law Bulletin, August 1993.

## SUMMARY PROCEDURE

**4.20** In summary procedure the normal procedure is for the trial court to hear any disputed evidence under reservation as to competency so that the question of law can, if necessary, be examined by the High Court on appeal.[1] This procedure is equally applicable to confession evidence. In *Carmichael v Boyd*[2] the sheriff, following a defence objection, had refused to hear evidence of a police interview which he regarded as 'tainted' by certain questioning about a matter with which the accused had previously been charged. The High Court made it clear that he should not have upheld the objection to the effect of excluding a whole chapter of evidence and the case was remitted to the sheriff to hear the evidence.

1 *Clark v Stuart* 1949 SLT 461; *Renton and Brown* para 14–61.
2 1993 SCCR 751.

# 5. The evidential sufficiency of confessions in Scots law

## INTRODUCTION – THE REQUIREMENT FOR CORROBORATION

**5.01**  Scots criminal law generally sets a higher standard of sufficiency then other adversarial systems, including that of England. In the Scottish context it has been said that the requirement of corroboration in the law acknowledges the risk posed by the human fallibility of the fact-finding process, a risk which may be double: the fallibility of the witness himself and the fallibility of the tribunal which holds the witness to be credible.[1] On the other hand, in English law it is a general rule that the court may act on the uncorroborated testimony of one witness and such requirements as there are concerning a plurality of witnesses or some other confirmation of individual testimony are exceptional.[2]

1 Anon 'Corroboration of Evidence in Scottish Criminal Law' 1958 SLT (News) 137. See also *Hammond v Western SMT* 1968 unreported, quoted in Macphail *Evidence* § 23.02.
2 *Cross on Evidence* (7th edn) p 224.

**5.02**  It is important to realise that English texts dealing with corroboration require to be treated with care since English law tends to use the term 'corroboration' in a somewhat narrower, more technical sense than is the case in Scotland, and in certain situations where Scots law would consider that corroboration exists, notably the 'special knowledge' confession, English law would take a different view.[1]

1 Mirfield *Confessions* pp 203–206.

**5.03**  It was an ancient rule of Scots law that the testimony of a single witness was insufficient: 'Probatioun allanerlie be ane witness, is not sufficient of the law; *Quoniam in ore duorum aut trium stat omne verbum*'.[1] *Hume* explains the requirement for corroboration in the following terms:

'No matter how trivial the offence, and how high soever the credit and character of the witness, still our law is averse to rely on his single word, in any inquiry which may affect the person, liberty or fame of his neighbour; and rather than run the risk of such an error, a risk which does not hold when there is a concurrence of testimonies, it is willing that the guilty should escape.'[2]

1 Balfour *Practicks* 373.
2 Hume *Commentaries* II, 383.


**5.04**  Although substantial inroads have been made into this principle in civil matters, it remains a major rule of Scottish criminal evidence that crucial facts should be corroborated:

'No person can be convicted of a crime or statutory offence, except where the legislature otherwise directs, unless there is evidence of at least two witnesses implicating the person accused with the commission of the crime or offence with which he is charged.'[1]

The reference to 'two witnesses' in this celebrated quotation is perhaps slightly misleading and the point is rather more accurately stated by *Renton and Brown*:

'The basic requirement is that the offence be brought home to the accused by evidence from at least two sources. The question is not whether each of the several circumstances points by itself to guilt of the charge libelled, but whether taken together they are capable of supporting the inference of guilt beyond reasonable doubt.'[2]

1 *Morton v HM Advocate* 1938 JC 50 at 55 per Lord Justice-Clerk Aitchison.
2 *Criminal Procedure According to the Law of Scotland* para 18–52.


**5.05**  In modern Scots law the facts to be corroborated will vary according to the circumstances of the case, although the fact (a) that a crime has been committed and (b) that the accused in the dock committed it are always crucial and will, unless statute provides otherwise, require corroboration.[1]

1 Walker and Walker *The Law of Evidence in Scotland* p 405, § 383.


**5.06**  With the sole exception of a recorded plea of guilty, this principle applies to confessions as much as to any other type of evidence, a point recently re-emphasised in *Meredith v Lees*.[1] In the case of a confession, the corroboration must come from an independent source and a confession is not corroborated by being heard by two or more people. Although this point first arose in *Banaghan v HM Advocate*[2] it was not decided and it is surprising that it was as late as 1988 before the issue was resolved. In *Bainbridge v Scott*[3] it was made clear that a confession is not corroborated by being repeated, even in different terms and to different witnesses. Conversely, if the requisite corroboration is available from an independent source, (ie if the confession is not of the 'special knowledge' variety) it is not necessary that the confession itself should be spoken to by more than one witness.[4]

1 1992 SCCR 459 at 462E.
2 (1888) 1 White 566.
3 1988 SLT 871.
4 *Innes v HM Advocate* 1955 SLT (Notes) 69; cf *Low v HM Advocate* 1993 SCCR 493.

**5.07** There is sometimes confusion between a confession of the commission of a crime and a statement by an accused as to his intention. In the latter case, in order to be sufficient evidence of intention on its own, the making of the statement requires to be corroborated. However, if it is corroborated no further evidence of intention is required. Thus in *Normand v Matthews*[1] two police officers gave evidence that the accused had been found in possession of a knife and had said that he needed it 'for protection'. The sheriff held this insufficient for conviction on a charge under section 1 of the Prevention of Crimes Act 1953 since it was only a single adminicle of evidence from a single source. This decision was overturned on appeal, the High Court holding explicitly that where there is evidence from two witnesses of a statement by the accused of his intention, that is sufficient evidence of his intention for any purpose for which his intention may be relevant.

1 1993 SCCR 856.


# A HISTORY OF 'JUDICIAL' CONFESSIONS

**5.08** The earliest mention of confessions in Scots law can be found in Balfour's *Practicks*[1] where it is stated that 'Confessioun maid in judgment and accepit be ony persoun havand interes thairanent, or be ane uther in his name, is prejudicial to the maker thairof, and makis sufficient probatioun and faith aganis him in all things that ar confessit'.

1 381, cl.

**5.09** The first clear discussion of confessions in early Scots criminal law, as opposed to *Balfour*'s bald statement of principle, appears in *Mackenzie*.[1] For him a 'judicial' confession means a confession emitted before the judges who are sitting in judgment on the pannel. He describes the pannel's judicial confession as 'the most secure' means of proof. However, even at this early date Scots law was concerned to avoid the possibility of a false confession and if there were any doubts about the genuineness of the confession or the accused's state of mind, the confession, though not rendered inadmissible, had to be supported by other evidence:

'But because Men will sometimes confess a Crime, rather out of Weariness of their Life, than a Consciousness of Guilt; therefore the Law hath required, that if there appear any Aversion for Life, *tedium vitae*, or any Sings of Distraction or Madness, that these Confessions should not be relied upon, except they be adminiculated with other Probation.'

1 *Works* p 249.

**5.10**  *Mackenzie* asserts that 'such as confess are oft-times condemned without the knowledge of an inquest' ie without being remitted to a jury. However, on closer examination this assertion is only supported by two cases, both involving special circumstances,[1] and, if such a practice existed, (which *Hume* doubts) it was restricted to non-capital cases. According to *Hume*[2] it was a long-established rule of Scottish procedure that a confession of guilt was not of itself sufficient to permit the court to proceed to sentence.

1 *Rutherford's Case* 9 July 1622; *Job's Case* 19 January 1650.
2 II, 320.

**5.11**  From about 1665 onwards this applied even where the confession was made in open court before the full assize. What was required was a confession to the actual jury chosen to try the case. Thus, notwithstanding that the accused had pled guilty before the whole assize, a jury still had to be chosen, and the accused was required to renew his plea before it and it was required to return a verdict convicting him before sentence could be passed. If the accused changed his mind and withdrew his confession or refused to renew his plea before the jury, the matter had to proceed to trial and the jury was entitled to acquit the accused if it considered it appropriate. In special circumstances, even where the confession had been repeated to the jury, the prosecutor might decide to strengthen the case against the accused by leading further evidence, although *Hume* states that this was uncommon.[1]

1 II, 320.

**5.12**  Apart from confessions made in its presence, practice seems to have varied over the years as to exactly what sort of confession was sifficient to entitle a jury to convict.[1] It also has to be borne in mind that many of the early cases are political in nature and, before the High Court of Justiciary was founded in 1672, the Privy Council was wont to interfere with the administration of justice by the Justiciars.[2]

1 See generally *Hume* II, 321–323.
2 *Hume* II, 27 ff.

**5.13** *Mackenzie* and *Hume* refer to a number of seventeenth-century cases where confessions to magistrates, clergymen, Privy Councillors and even judges outwith the presence of an assize were all held to be sufficient. Confessions to magistrates, clergymen and the like had to be proved in court but those to Privy Councillors or the Lords of Justiciary which had been reduced to writing were held 'judicial' and to prove themselves. Such did not require to be spoken to by witnesses although on one occasion a remarkably independently-minded jury acquitted a prisoner in the face of two declarations, one emitted before the Lords of Justiciary, because 'they did neither hear the party confess the said crymes, nor the alleadged confession of the pannel, given in for probation thereof, owned be the pannel, nor otherwise proven'.[1] There were doubts about the correctness of relying on such confessions, and particularly on the question of when a confession was 'judicial'. The Act 1685 c10 finally laid down that declarations before Privy Councillors were only 'judicial' in the case of treason and only then if emitted after the service of the indictment.

1 *James Douglas* (1682) Hume II 322.

**5.14** *Mackenzie* describes the embryonic judicial declaration procedure thus:

'The custom with us is that the Advocate doth, in Presence of the Justices, examine the party to be accused, and if he confess, either he subscribes his Confession, if he can write, or else the Justices subscribe for him, or which is securer, make two Notars and four Witnesses subscribe; . . .'.

Evidence of the confession might then be led at the trial. The practice was not entirely consistent and examples may be found of confessions in declarations emitted at judicial examination being treated as 'judicial, irretractable, sole and conclusive evidence of the pannel's guilt, as if emitted to the assize themselves'. However, it was argued that the use of a declaration in this way offended against the Act 1587 c 91 which required 'the haill accusatioun, ressoning, writtis, witnesses and utheris probatioun and instructioun quhatsumeuer of the cryme salbe allegit ressonit and deducit to the assyse in the presence of the party accusit in face of iudgement and in no utheris wayes'.[1]

1 *Finlay McNab* 7 December 1669; Mackenzie *Works* p 249; Erskine *Institute* IV, iv, 96.

**5.15** By Hume's time it was settled law that while a declaration was admissible against the prisoner, it required to be acknowledged by him or proved by witnesses and any confession which it contained was not conclusive. Such a confession was nevertheless a circumstance 'of no mean weight' in the prosecution case.[1]

1 *Hume* II, 324 ff.

**5.16** There is also early precedent for the admission of a declaration emitted in connection with a civil matter as evidence against the accused in a criminal trial.[1]

1 *Maciver and Maccallum* (1784) Hume II 326.

## HISTORY OF 'NON-JUDICIAL' VERBAL CONFESSIONS

**5.17** For the earliest statement of the law it is once again necessary to refer to *Balfour*[1] who quotes the case of *Andro Rutherfurd contra James Dempster* in 1559 as authority for the proposition that:

'Confessioun maid be ony man outwith judgment, and instrument tane thairupon is sufficient probatioun aganis the maker thairof in judgment; as gif ony man havand ony gudis or geir in his possessioun confessit the samin to appertene to ane uther, and the uther or ony in his name, tak instruments thairupon, the samin preivis sufficientlie that the gudis pertenis to that uther.'

1 381, c 1.

**5.18** Balfour's statement would appear to refer to a civil matter rather than a criminal one, although it should of course be borne in mind that at this period there was not the same clear-cut distinction between civil and criminal matters as there is today. Attempts to elucidate the early Scottish practice are further hampered by the fact that once again *Mackenzie* and *Hume* disagree. The former states that:

'because Confessions are oft-times emitted negligently, the Confessors thinking that their private Confessions cannot prejudge them, therefore the Law doth only give Credit to judicial Confessions, and not to these that are extrajudicial, and *extra bancum* which Maxim is stronger with us, than elsewhere, because by a particular Act of Parliament, *James VI Parl, ii cap 90* all Probation should be led in presence of the Assize.'[1]

1 Page 249.

**5.19** *Hume*, who regarded extra-judicial confessions as a form of circumstantial evidence, states that it was always Scottish custom to allow proof of verbal confessions of guilt made at or near the time of the crime although the evidential value of such confessions was less than that of those which were reduced to writing, and made with more solemnity and deliberation:

'In a case of theft, if on being seized with the stolen goods upon him, the thief instantly confess his crime, and offer back the goods, or tempt the owner with a bribe to let him go; or in a case of murder, if the killer be taken red-hand, and brought into the presence of the dying man, and there lament his rashness, and ask forgiveness of his victim: Such incidents are not mere words of acknowledgment; they are links in the chain of circumstance, and equally bear evidence against the pannel, as blood on his clothes, or the goods found concealed on his person.'

Confessions of this nature which were intimately connected with the crime were to be taken into consideration and assessed in the circumstances of each individual case. Such evidence was obviously weighty and *Hume* quotes many examples although he disapproves of one case where the accused was hanged for murder solely on the basis of confessions to bystanders and the finding of the body of the deceased.[1]

1 *Hume* II, 333.

## MODERN PRACTICE – JUDICIAL CONFESSIONS

### Plea of guilty

**5.20**   The requirement to remit to a jury a charge to which the prisoner pled guilty was abolished by the Act 9 Geo IV c 29, section 14[1] and in modern practice a formal, recorded plea of guilty which is accepted by the prosecution is conclusive evidence of the accused's guilt. If, as is generally the case, the plea is tendered before a jury has been empannelled, the judge will proceed to sentence without any further consideration of the sufficiency of the evidence. Prior to the passing of the Prisoners and Criminal Proceedings (Scotland) Act 1993 if the plea was tendered and/or accepted after a jury had been empannelled it was directed by the judge to return a verdict of guilty in terms of the accused's confession. Nowadays the jury no longer has any function in relation to a plea tendered and accepted by the Crown after it has been empannelled. Such a plea will now simply be accepted by the judge.[2]

1 See Alison *Practice* 367–369.
2 Criminal Procedure (Scotland) Act 1975, s 137A(2) inserted by the Prisoners and Criminal Proceedings (Scotland) Act 1993, Sch 5.

### The danger of the false guilty plea

**5.21**   Since the time of Mackenzie, Scots law has been anxious to avoid the possibility of a conviction following a false confession or a false plea of guilty. Among the text writers, Dickson in particular stresses the dangers of the false confession, ie a freely-made confession by a person who did not commit the crime.[1]

1 Dickson *The Law of Evidence in Scotland* pp 263–265, §§ 380–384. None of the examples given arose in Scotland.

**5.22**  Although under modern circumstances the danger of a false confessor reaching the court is slender the possibility cannot be ignored and the one known modern Scottish example involved not merely a false confession to the police but also a false plea of guilty tendered under the accelerated procedure of section 102 of the Criminal Procedure (Scotland) Act 1975. This extraordinary case, *Boyle v HM Advocate*,[1] concerned a deserter from the forces who was being escorted into military custody, when he produced from his pocket a newspaper cutting about a serious bank robbery and told his military escort that he had committed the crime. They immediately returned him to police custody and he then proceeded to make to the police a 'detailed and circumstantial confession' to the crime. The confession would appear to have been based on litle more than the newspaper report but nevertheless with legal advice Boyle subsequently submitted a section 102 letter and having pled guilty he was sentenced to nine years' imprisonment. Boyle's bizarre behaviour appears to have been motivated by a desire to avoid a period in military custody. The nine years' imprisonment must have been an unpleasant surprise and he belatedly sought to have the conviction quashed. The report is largely concerned with the procedural issues, but it should be noted that the Crown, which appears to have acted in good faith throughout, conceded that Boyle was wholly innocent and that there had indeed been a miscarriage of justice, and this concession was clearly a major factor in persuading the High Court to quash the conviction. Lord Cameron stated the self-evident when he commented that 'for the predicament in which he finds himself, however, the applicant must bear a heavy responsibility for his deliberate, detailed and repeated false admissions and confession' and it remains to be seen what attitude the High Court will adopt if a similar situation arises again but without the important concession by the Crown.

1 1976 SLT 126.

**5.23**  At summary level an accused person who pleads guilty with legal advice can expect scant sympathy from the High Court if the plea turns out to have been wrongly tendered, certainly if there is no concession by the Crown that there has been a miscarriage of justice.[1]

1 *MacGregor v MacNeill* 1975 JC 57; *Pirie v McNaughton* 1991 SCCR 483.

**5.24** There has also been at least one example of an accused person pleading guilty in a situation where no crime, or certainly not the crime with which he was charged, had been committed.[1] The accused had pled guilty to various charges of incest and other related offences with a girl believed by all concerned, including the accused and the girl herself, to be his daughter. He was later charged with other offences relating to the same girl but by this time science had moved on and the evidence was subjected to DNA testing which established conclusively that he could not have been the girl's father. The earlier conviction was quashed, once again with the consent of the Crown. The circumstances were clearly wholly exceptional and this might more appropriately be described as a confession tendered under essential error rather than a false confession.[2]

1 *Herald* 6 October 1990, briefly reported as *M v HM Advocate* 1990 GWD 37–2106.
2 See also *Dickson* p 265, § 383.

## Judicial declaration and judicial examination

**5.25** Historically, the legal effect of a confession in a judicial declaration was regarded as similar to that of an extra-judicial confession.[1] Although obviously a matter of considerable weight, a confession in a judicial declaration was never regarded as conclusive evidence and required to be corroborated by evidence from another source.[2] The mere proof of the commission of the crime was insufficient to provide corroboration; there had to be some evidence connecting the accused with the crime.[3] It was a question of facts and circumstances in each case what additional evidence would be sufficient to provide corroboration but a merely suspicious circumstance, such as hiding from apprehension, was not enough.[4]

1 *Walker and Walker* p 29.
2 *Hume* II, 324; *Alison* 578; *Dickson* p 238, § 339. *Archibald Duncan and Charles Mackenzie* (1831) Bell's Notes 239; *Banaghan v HM Advocate* (1888) 1 White 566.
3 *Dunlop* (1823) *Alison* 578–579 and authorities in previous note.
4 Macdonald *The Criminal Law of Scotland* p 334. *Ann Duff and Janet Falconer* (1831) Bell's Notes 239; *James Douglas* (1834) Bell's Notes 240; *John Buchanan* (1837) Bell's Notes 240.

**5.26** *Dickson* observed that prisoners were 'every day convicted upon confessions in their declarations, corroborated by circumstances which throw considerable suspicion upon them but which would not of themselves prove the prosecutor's case'. *Dickson* considered this just and commented that 'a false confession in a declaration is very rare and unlikely, indeed, not many degrees less so than a false plea of guilty' although as we now know such a situation can arise. In the age before the tape-recorder, *Dickson* also warned against the possibility of the statement not having been taken down in the prisoner's precise words, its precise meaning thus being misconceived, and he observed that an intentional misstatement was not impossible.[1]

1 *Dickson* p 261, § 376.

**5.27**   The question of sufficiency has not yet arisen in connection with the Criminal Justice (Scotland) Act 1980 procedures but it is thought that the courts will apply the general principles of corroboration of extra-judicial confessions.


## The evidence of the accused

**5.28**   Since the pannel was not competent to give evidence in his own defence prior to the Criminal Evidence Act 1898, there is no early authority on the question of a confession made in the course of the accused's evidence.

**5.29**   In *Drysdale v Adair*[1] an accused on trial for assault admitted in evidence that he had struck a blow but explained that it had been done in self-defence. The sheriff-substitute took the accused's admission as corroboration of the fact of the assault, but rejected the evidence of self-defence and convicted. On appeal the High Court held that corroboration might be obtained from the evidence of the accused without his entire evidence being believed. The report of *Drysdale v Adair* is extremely brief. However, a much fuller report is available of *McArthur v Stewart*[2] in which the High Court held that where, in the course of giving evidence at his trial, the accused admits a crucial fact which was only spoken to by one Crown witness, his evidence will provide a necessary corroboration. This point also arose, inconclusively, in *Miln v Whaley*.[3] In *McArthur v Stewart* the possibility of a prosecutor taking up a case without sufficient evidence in the hope of securing an admission from the assused was deplored by Lord Carmont and in modern practice the 'no case to answer' provisions of the 1975 Act[4] will operate to terminate the case before the question of the accused giving evidence arises.

1 1947 SLT (Notes) 63.
2 1955 SLT 434.
3 1975 SLT (Notes) 75.
4 Sections 140A and 345A.


**5.30**   Lord Cameron has expressed the view that an admission of guilt by the accused in the witness box is conclusive.[1] However, there are no cases and a different view is taken by *Renton and Brown*[2] which states that an admission on oath in the witness box must be corroborated by evidence from another source. While it is respectfully suggested that *Renton and Brown's* view is in accordance with principle and correct, in modern practice the question is not likely to be of much practical importance since the Crown will have had to lead at least sufficient evidence to overcome a 'no case to answer' submission[3] before the question of the accused going into the witness box will arise.

1 'Scottish Practice in Relation to Admissions and Confessions by Persons Suspected or Accused of Crime' 1975 SLT 265.
2 Para 18–59.
3 1975 Act, ss 140A and 345A.

**5.31** In *Ward v HM Advocate*[1] the accused had been charged with murder. He had admitted assaulting the deceased by punching and kicking him to severe injury both to the police and at judicial examination and he had given evidence to that effect at the trial. Having been convicted of assault to severe injury he sought to claim that he had only admitted assault for fear of being convicted of murder and he also claimed that there had been no corroboration of his admission. The High Court refused the appeal and held *inter alia* that it was now too late for the accused to withdraw his admission since there had been no dispute at the trial that it had been made to the police and at judicial examination and it had been repeated on oath before the jury. It had, in effect, become a judicial admission of guilt.

1 1993 GWD 9–590.

### Other judicial proceedings

**5.32** It is thought that an admission of guilt in judicial proceedings other than the accused's own trial, such as civil proceedings or a fatal accident inquiry, would be treated on the same basis as an extrajudicial confession and hence would require corroboration in accordance with the normal principles.[1]

1 Cf *Banaghan v HM Advocate* (1888) 1 White 566.

## EXTRA-JUDICIAL CONFESSIONS

### The general principles

**5.33** As already noted it has long been the law in Scotland that an extra-judicial confession is not of itself full proof of guilt and must be corroborated by other evidence, either direct or circumstantial, throwing suspicion on the prisoner.[1] It is impossible, given the infinite variety of forms which such confessions can take, to lay down with any precision the amount or nature of corroborative evidence required. Each case must depend on its own facts. However, the evidence tendered as corroboration must incriminate the accused and must, taken along with the terms of the confession, be sufficient to establish beyond reasonable doubt the accused's guilt of the charge. Where all that is proved is the confession and the commission of the crime, this is insufficient, since proof of the crime merely establishes that it was committed by someone and does not corroborate the accused's confession that he committed it.[2] It is the contents of the confession which must be corroborated. Thus, where corroboration comes from an outside source the making of the confession need only be spoken to by one witness.[3] On the other hand, where the corroboration comes from the terms of the confession itself (ie the 'special knowledge' situation) the making of the confession must be spoken to by more than one witness in order to be sufficient on its own.[4]

1 *Hume* II, 333; *Dickson* p 245, § 352; *Walker and Walker* p 29.
2 *Connolly v HM Advocate* 1958 SLT 79 at 81 per Lord Patrick and Lord Mackintosh.
3 *Mills v HM Advocate* 1935 JC 77; *Innes v HM Advocate* 1955 SLT (Notes) 69.
4 *Low v HM Advocate* 1993 SCCR 493.


**5.34**  Of the older Scottish writers, *Dickson* offers by far the fullest treatment of the probative value of extra-judicial admissions and confessions.[1] He sets out two basic points which require attention in assessing admissions and confessions: (a) the medium through which the supposed admission or confession comes before the jury; and (b) the motives which may have induced the party to make it and the circumstances under which it may have been emitted.

1 Page 261, § 375 ff.


**5.35**  *Dickson* stresses the need for caution in assessing the evidence or oral admissions and confessions.[1] Many of the pointers which he suggests continue to be appropriate under modern conditions. Thus, the jury ought always to be satisfied of the opportunity for observation of the accuracy and memory and the veracity of the witness before they attach any weight to his evidence. *Dickson* quotes with approval a dictum of Baron Parke in the English case of *Earle v Picken*:[2]

'It very frequently happens not only that the witness has misunderstood what the party has said, but that by unintentionally altering a few of the expressions really used, he gives an effect to the statement completely at variance with what the party really did say.'

Only part of the statement may have been heard, and important qualifications unnoticed or forgotten. The accused and the witness may
have attached different meanings to an ambiguous or inaccurate
expression. *Dickson* also stresses the need for the witness to repeat the
accused's words verbatim rather than his own inference from them
and cites an unreported case, *E Dow*,[3] in which the accused was
indicted for theft of a shawl. A police officer deponed that the accused
'confessed' but under cross-examination conceded that all she had
said was that she 'had taken the shawl'. The accused was acquitted on
the basis that she lacked theftous intent. It follows that it is important to bring out as nearly as possible the actual expressions which
were used and the jury should disregard any such general statement,
as that the party 'confessed' or 'admitted'.

1 Page 261, § 377 ff.
2 (1833) 5 C & P 542.
3 Perth Spring Circuit, 1850.

**5.36** Dickson is unequivocal in his views on the danger of fabricated
confessions. The present writer is unaware of any proven modern
example of the outright fabrication of a confession by a Scottish police
officer and standards of policing have improved beyond recognition
since Dickson's day. Nevertheless, recent events in England make the
passage worth quoting in full for its prophetic ring:

'Evidence of oral admissions is also easily fabricated, and the chance of
detecting its untruth is small; for when all a witness speaks to is an independent
statement, his falsehood is almost beyond the reach of cross-examination, and
is seldom contradictory to the proved circumstances attending the crime. Peculiar caution is always necessary when the person repeating the supposed confession is an officer engaged in the pursuit of criminals for such persons are apt to
be biassed witnesses, and to attribute a guilty meaning to ambiguous, and even
to harmless acts and words, of persons whom they apprehend.'[1]

1 *Dickson* p 262, § 378.

**5.37** Despite these strictures, and his views on the dangers of false
confessions, Dickson lays the foundation for the modern view of confessions when he observes:

'Extra-judicial confessions . . . (if distinctly proved), are usually entitled to
much weight, and strong corroborative evidence will not be required to
complete the proof of guilt. The peculiar value of confessional evidence lies in
its furnishing the best proof of the intention which constitutes the essence of
most crimes.'[1]

Provided appropriate caution is exercised, the risk of a confession
being untrue ought not to be exaggerated:

'If, on careful investigation, the statement is found to be distinctly sworn to by an accurate and credible witness, to be free from any appearance of disturbing motive or misconception in the party, and to be in unison with the other evidence in the case, it ought to receive effect as evidence of a highly trustworthy character.'[2]

1 *Dickson* p 262, § 379.
2 Ibid p 265, § 384.

## Case law – the 'unequivocal confession'

**5.38** The first clear, reported judicial statement that a confession was insufficient on its own appears to have been in 1838 in the case of *Thomas Hunter*[1] but it is surprising how little case law there was on sufficiency until comparatively recently. The most important of the earlier cases are summarised by *Macdonald*.[2] The clearest, and still the most authoritative, case on the point is *Connolly v HM Advocate*[3] which, for some reason, was not reported until almost three years after it was decided. Although *Connolly* contains elements of what would today be regarded as a 'special knowledge' confession, that issue would have to wait until *Manuel v HM Advocate*[4] for full consideration from the High Court and *Connolly* is primarily an authority on general principles.

1 (1838) Bell's Notes 239.
2 *The Criminal Law of Scotland* (5th edn) p 334.
3 1958 SLT 79.
4 1958 JC 41; para 5.67 below.

**5.39** The circumstances in *Connolly* were straightforward. The accused was seen by some civilians to be sitting in a car, late at night, apparently just hanging around. The civilians were suspicious and reported the matter to the police. The accused was taken to the police station (on what basis is not clear) and the police returned to the car and stood by it until two men, White and Thomson, came round the corner from a street called Rosefield Avenue. On seeing the police White made off and Thomson spoke to the officers for a few moments before also taking to his heels. Later the same night a quantity of stolen goods was found in a house in Rosefield Avenue. In the police station Connolly made a statement, described as 'circumstantial and detailed', describing how he and Thomson had broken into a shop and transported the stolen property to the house in Rosefield Avenue. He was convicted after trial and appealed. The High Court, Lord Justice-Clerk Thomson, Lord Partick and Lord Mackintosh, rejected the appeal.

**5.40**  Lord Thomson set out the general principles of the law in what remains a classic statement:

'It is a fundamental rule of our criminal law that no-one can be convicted on the evidence of one witness and that there must be testimony incriminating the accused derived from two separate sources. It is consistent with that rule, though whether it is derived from it is not certain, that no accused can be convicted on his own confession alone. A confession of guilt – short of a formal plea of guilty – is not enough. There must be evidence from some other source which incriminates the accused. If all that the Crown can produce is evidence – however complete and exhaustive – that a crime has been committed together with evidence, however credible, that the accused confessed to having committed it, the Crown must fail. There must be something incriminatory of the accused spoken to by someone other than the accused. While it is necessary that there should be evidence from two independent sources, the weight to be attached to each source may vary. If one source is unimpeachable, the standard required of the other may be lower than if the first source carries less weight. It is the conjunction of the testimonies which is important.'

His Lordship side-stepped the question of the special knowledge issue and stated that he found corroboration in the circumstances, viz the presence of the accused in the car, alone for an hour in the vicinity of the place where the stolen goods were found at a time which would fit in with the theft, and the conduct of White and Thomson when they saw the police. According to his Lordship, while this was not very strong evidence, when it was put alongside the confession, the two in combination were 'irresistible'.

**5.41**  Lord Justice-Clerk Thomson again presided over the High Court when their Lordships dealt with *Sinclair v Clark*.[1] This road-traffic case marks the first appearance of the High Court's frequently repeated view that the corroborative evidence need only 'afford a sufficient independent check of [an] unequivocal admission' in order to satisfy the requirements of the law. Lord Thomson's judgment is also of interest in that it shows, quite overtly, his Lordship calling in question the requirement for a confession to be corroborated at all:

'There is a rule in our law – a somewhat archaic rule – the merit of which under modern conditions is not always obvious, at all events where the admission is beyond suspicion – that short of a solemn plea of guilt, an admission of guilt by an accused is not conclusive against him unless it is corroborated by something beyond the actual admission. One reason for this rule is to ensure that there is nothing phoney or quixotic about the confession. What is required in the way of independent evidence in order to elide such a risk must depend on the facts of the case, and in particular the nature and character of the confession and the circumstances under which it is made.'

1  1963 SLT 307.

**5.42** In so far as 'phoney and quixotic' means anything at all, it appears that his Lordship was considering the possibility of a confession by a person who had not committed the crime, a false confessor. The importance of the requirement for corroboration as a protection for the accused against possible police malpractice does not appear to have occurred to his Lordship. Admittedly it was to be some years before 'verballing' by the police became a perceived problem, but his Lordship's *obiter* comments show how far the pendulum had swung since Dickson's time.

**5.43** The 'sufficient independent check' test was explicitly reiterated in *Keane v Horn*.[1] In addition, following *Sinclair v Clark* there has been a series of road traffic cases concerning corroboration of the accused's admission of driving in which the High Court has repeatedly stated its view that very little is required to corroborate an 'unequivocal admission'.[2]

1 (1978) SCCR Supp 225.
2 The other cases in the series are *Torrance v Thaw* 1970 JC 58; *Lodhi v Skeen* (1978) SCCR Supp 197; *Miln v Fitzgerald* (1978) SCCR Supp 205; *McDonald v Smith* (1978) SCCR Supp 219; *MacNab v Culligan* (1978) SCCR Supp 222 and *Lockhart v Crockett* 1986 SCCR 685. None of them contribute anything material to the development of the law and they are not discussed individually. Reference may also be made to *Sinclair v MacLeod* 1964 JC 19 where in special circumstances a conviction was overturned despite an unequivocal admission in response to a police requirement.

**5.44** *Sinclair v Clark* has also been cited many times outwith the context of road traffic law, notably in *Hartley v HM Advocate*[1] where, although the circumstances surrounding the making of the confession were rather dubious, it was accepted the confession was clearly unequivocal and was held to require very little corroboration. Although *Connolly* was not cited in *Hartley*, it is noteworthy that in the latter case Lord Grieve, who of the three judges considers the question of sufficiency most fully, referred to the requirement of corroboration being met by 'something [which] must point to the accused as the perpetrator of the crime to which he has confessed', a considerably lower standard than Lord Justice-Clerk Thomson's statement in *Connolly* that there had to be evidence from two sources which *incriminated* the accused.

1 1979 SLT 26 (with correction noted at 300).

**5.45** In Lord Dunpark's opinion confession evidence had a special status:

'The standard of corroboration of an unequivocal confession of guilt is, in my opinion, different from the standard to be applied when seeking corroboration of a Crown eyewitness at a criminal trial or of the evidence of a pursuer or defender in a civil case. The reason for the different standard is that, unlike such other evidence the confession of guilt by an accused person is prejudicial to his own interests and may, therefore, initially be assumed to be true. Accordingly, one is not then looking for extrinsic evidence which is more consistent with his guilt than with his innocence, but for extrinsic evidence which is consistent with his confession of guilt. If, therefore, a jury is satisfied that a confession of guilt was freely made and unequivocal in its terms, corroboration of that confession may be found in evidence from another source or sources which point to the truth of the confession.'

**5.46**  *Hartley* is an unsatisfactory case from many points of view, not least the total failure to address the issue of the protection of the accused. In *Meredith v Lees*[1] the High Court reviewed a number of the earlier authorities including *Sinclair v Clark* itself and the Lord Justice-Clerk took the opportunity to make it clear that the amount of evidence required to corroborate an unequivocal confession would depend on circumstances. His Lordship restated the 'fundamental rule . . . that no-one who confesses to a crime, unless by a formal plea of guilty, can be convicted solely on his own confession. There must be evidence from some other source which *incriminates* the accused'.[2] After noting that it had often been said that if there is a clear and unequivocal admission of guilt, then very little evidence in corroboration of such an admission is required, his Lordship went on:

'But it is not appropriate that this approach to what is required to corroborate a clear and unequivocal confession should be described as a rule. A confession may be clear and unequivocal in its terms, yet the circumstances in which it was made may leave room for doubt as to whether it can be relied upon. There is a risk that, by describing the requirement in minimal terms by using words such as "very little" and then elevating it into a rule, there will be a weakenng of the principle that there must be a sufficient independent check of the confession to corroborate it.'

1 1992 SCCR 459.
2 This passage can be contrasted with Lord Grieve's opinion in *Hartley* quoted in para 5.44 above.

**5.47**  One issue which has produced differing conclusions from the High Court is the requirement to prove the commission of the crime to which the accused has confessed. In *Sinclair v Tudhope*[1] the accused was found by police officers in Miller Street, Glasgow concealing something in the front of his anorak and looking about in a suspicious manner. He was stopped and found to be in possession of three diaries. Under caution he made an unequivocal admission to the theft of the diaries from a named shop in Miller Street. There was evidence that the recovered diaries were similar to diaries stocked by that shop but the High Court took the view that this was insufficient to prove that any theft of diaries, let alone the actual ones recovered, had taken place. In the circumstances the conviction was quashed, although the High Court did comment on how near the Crown had come to success and implied that things might have been different if the accused had been seen to come out of the shop or if there had been evidence that the diaries were unlikely to have been obtained anywhere else.

1  1987 SCCR 690.

**5.48**  It is difficult to reconcile this decision with the briefly-reported case of *Allan v Hamilton*[1] (which was not cited in argument) in which once again the only evidence of the commission of a crime would appear to have come from the accused's own admission but the conviction was upheld.

1  1972 SLT (Notes) 2.

**5.49**  Although *Sinclair v Tudhope* has not been overruled, its authority must now be regarded as doubtful following the decision to distinguish it in *McVeigh v Normand*[1] despite several close similarities. In this case the accused was found in possession of certain items of clothing. She was coming from the general direction of a Littlewoods store, although some distance from it. She made an unequivocal admission to the theft of the clothing but she did not say where she had obtained it. The items were identified as being exclusively stocked by Littlewoods, although not by any specific branch, and there does not appear to have been any evidence of a theft having occurred at the nearby branch. Nevertheless a conviction for stealing the items from that particular shop was upheld.

1  1992 SCCR 272.

## Case law – equivocal confession

**5.50**  Several cases have addressed the question of the statement which is either not clearly an admission of the crime charged or not even clearly a confession at all. In *Tudhope v Dalgleish*[1] the accused's car had allegedly collided with a parked vehicle and failed to stop. When the police arrived at the accused's house, apparently fairly soon after the accident, they found that her car was parked outside showing signs of recent accident damage (although nothing that could be related to the parked vehicle) and with the engine still warm. Under section 168 of the Road Traffic Act 1972 police asked the accused who had been driving the car when it was involved in a road traffic accident, to which she replied, 'I was driving it a short time ago'.

1  1986 SCCR 559.

**5.51** In what was surely a narrow decision, the sheriff acquitted on the basis that the Crown had failed to set up either an accident involving the accused or an admission by her and on appeal his decision was upheld, the High Court observing:

'. . . the respondent was . . . asked who had been driving the vehicle when it was involved in a road traffic accident, her reply was not that she had been driving when an accident had occurred but that she had been driving the vehicle a short time ago. In our opinion that statement cannot be regarded as a clear and unequivocal statement to the effect that she was the driver at the relevant time.'

**5.52** *Tudhope v Dalgleish* is very much a decision on its own facts and is clearly not of general application since it was distinguished in *Dunion v Cardle*.[1] In the latter case the accused was asked about the ownership of a car and replied that it was his and he had been driving it all day. This was held to be a clear and unequivocal admission that he had been driving when various offences were committed since it excluded the possibility of anyone else having been driving at the material time.

1  1993 GWD 3–153.

**5.53** In *Aiton v HM Advocate*[1] the accused was indicted for murder following a stabbing in a nightclub. The case against him was heavily dependent on two statements which it was alleged he had made and which amounted to implied admissions. These were firstly a remark to police officers, the day after he had been cautioned and charged, 'Ach, look I gave the knife to a man. It's destroyed', and secondly a statement to a civilian witness shortly after the incident to the effect that he (Aiton) had 'chibbed some guy'. There was other circumstantial evidence against him, particularly from a witness, Hart, who spoke to seeing Aiton stab somebody, although he could not identify the victim, but the statements were the mainstay of the prosecution case. In no sense could either of these statements be classified as an 'unequivocal admission' of the murder with which he was charged but nevertheless the Crown case was presented on the basis that they were the starting point of the evidence and the question was whether there was enough to corroborate them. The conviction was upheld on appeal.

1  1987 SCCR 252.

**5.54** In *Crowe v MacPhail*[1] the point in issue was whether the Crown had demonstrated that the accused had knowledge and control, and hence possession, of a piece of cannabis found in his prison cell. The cannabis was found in the ashtray appropriate to the accused's bed and when cautioned and charged by the police with possessing cannabis he replied 'It wasn't exactly in my possession. It was under my ashtray. There is a difference'. He was convicted after trial and the conviction was upheld on appeal.

1 1987 SLT (Notes) 316.

**5.55** *Sinclair v Clark* was again considered in *Greenshields v HM Advocate*[1] which was the first case to deal in any real depth with the question of an unclear and equivocal confession. Greenshields was indicted for a grisly murder which also involved the dismembering and burning of the victim's body. The problem for the courts arose at least partly from a bizarre decision by the police to charge him not only with murder but also with attempting to pervert the course of justice by dismembering the body. He replied 'You don't think I did it myself do you; but I'm telling you nothing about it until I see my lawyer'. At his trial the Crown relied on this statement as a confession to murder and sought corroboration in the finding of blood stains, certain other comments by the accused and evidence of his behaviour when interviewed by the police. However, the statement to the police was critical in providing a sufficiency of evidence. Defence counsel took the point that the reply could have related to either murder or attempting to pervert the course of justice or to both and it could have been consistent with the accused admitting that he assisted in the disposal of the body but no more.

1 1989 SCCR 637.

**5.56** While the appeal court agreed that the statement could not be regarded as a clear and unequivocal admission, the crucial question was whether the jury was entitled to regard it as an implied or equivocal admission of murder. The Lord Justice-Clerk put it thus:

'It is not only clear and unequivocal admissions which have evidential value. It has often been said that if there is a clear and unequivocal admission of guilt, then very little evidence in corroboration of such an admission is required. That is not to say, however, that something less than a clear and unequivocal admission is of no value. The first question must have been for the jury to determine whether the reply constituted an admission at all, and if so an admission of what. If the reply was capable of being treated as an admission, then the amount of evidence needed to corroborate that admission would depend on the circumstances of the case. . . . On the assumption that the reply was made, it was for the jury to determine whether the reply which the appellant made related to the attempt to pervert the course of justice only or whether it was a reply to the principal charge which was undoubtedly a charge of murder.'

**5.57** Although the trial had proceeded, and the trial judge had directed the jury on the basis that if the jury accepted the police evidence it was open to it to interpret it as an implied admission and then seek corroboration in the rest of the evidence, the Lord Justice-Clerk was of the view that this was not the only way, or even the best way, in which the case could have been presented. In his Lordship's view, the case was really one of circumstantial evidence with the alleged reply as a critical ingredient:

'[O]nce it is recognised that there was never any question of the reply being treated as an unequivocal or clear admission, and that the jury were left to determine whether they were satisfied that it constituted an implied admission, the sole question in the case became one of sufficiency of evidence. I regard the case as a classic one of circumstantial evidence; each of the matters relied upon individually may establish very little, but in conjunction with one another, the facts were in my opinion clearly sufficient to entitle the jury to convict the appellant of this charge.'

**5.58** The appeal court did not say that the trial judge was wrong, and thus there would appear to be two possible approaches to an equivocal admission. Firstly, the jury could be directed to look at the statement on its own, decide whether it is to be interpreted as a confession, and if so to what, and thereafter to seek corroboration in the other evidence. The problem with this approach, as Sheriff Gordon points out in his commentary, is the difficulty of separating the question of sufficiency of evidence from the question of weight of evidence since the corroboration needed for an equivocal confession is presumably greater than that required for an unequivocal one. The alternative approach, favoured by the Lord Justice-Clerk, is for the jury to regard the evidence as a whole and simply treat the reply as one source of evidence, an approach which certainly has the merit of simplicity and which is also consistent with *Hume's* view of the confession as circumstantial evidence.[1]

1 *Hume* II, 333.

*Circumstances peculiarly within the knowledge of the accused*

**5.59** In relation to matters such as driving without a licence or insurance or operating an unlicensed television set and the like, it is sufficient for conviction for the Crown, in the absence of contrary evidence, to lead evidence of an uncorroborated admission by the accused that he was unlicensed or uninsured. In such cases it is sufficient for the Crown to demonstrate *prima facie* the absence of entitlement to carry on the activity in question, the possession of a licence or an insurance certificate being facts peculiarly within the accused's knowledge.[1]

1 *Renton and Brown* para 18–54; *Miln v Whaley* 1975 SLT (Notes) 75 approving *John v Humphreys* [1955] 1 WLR 325 and *Davey v Towle* [1973] RTR 328; *Irving v Tudhope* 1987 SCCR 505.

## *Can the accused's demeanour provide corroboration?*

**5.60**  The only case to deal with this issue is *McGougan v HM Advocate*,[1] a case of child sex abuse, when it was held on consent by the Crown that the accused's demeanour and reactions when confronted both by the child's parents and the police could not be founded on as providing corroboration of his admissions, the logic of this presumably being that the reaction emanated from the same source as the admissions.

1 1991 SCCR 49.

## General principles – some observations

**5.61**  Although *Meredith v Lees*[1] is a welcome restatement of the basic issues involved in corroborating an unequivocal confession, and in particular of the requirement for there to be evidence from a second source which incriminates the accused, it would have been helpful if the High Court had gone rather further and undertaken a full review of the question of corroboration of confessions. *Meredith* leaves several strands hanging loose, particularly since the Lord Justice-Clerk brings the issues of admissibility and sufficiency into much closer conjunction than has hitherto been the position. On one view *Meredith* seems to be approaching the position that the trial court requires to decide for itself what it is about the confession that requires to be corroborated and how much corroboration is required in the circumstances. This may lay the law open to accusations of, in Sheriff Gordon's words, 'ad hoc-ery' and will make it difficult, at least until further guidance is given, for pleaders to determine the prospects of success in individual cases particularly if the confession falls between the two extremes of obviously unchallengable and obviously dubious. *Meredith* is most unlikely to be the final word on this issue.

1 1992 SCCR 459.

**5.62**    *Greenshields v HM Advocate*[1] is the first case to address the question of the equivocal confession, but the possibility of two different approaches which has been left unresolved means that it cannot at this stage be regarded as settling the law and it will be necessary to await further decisions before it becomes possible to identify any trends.

1 1989 SCCR 637.

## The 'special knowledge' confession

*The views of Alison*

**5.63**    The discussion so far has shown how little additional evidence is required to corroborate an unequivocal confession. Nevertheless, although the amount of evidence is slight, it must still come from outwith the terms of the confession itself. Parallel to the development of the general principles, the courts have developed the concept of what has colloquially become known as the 'special knowledge' confession, the basis of which is that the confession itself contains information which could only be known to the perpetrator of the crime. The 'special knowledge' confession is sometimes loosely referred to as being 'self-corroborating'. This term is theoretically (if not factually) inept and is avoided in the present work.

**5.64**    The first writer to articulate this principle was Alison whose statement remains, at least nominally, the basis of the modern 'special knowledge' rule:

'Confessions . . . come with most effect when they are connected, as is very frequently the case, with some articles of real evidence, which put it beyond a doubt that the statement given is in the main true. Thus, if a person is apprehended on a charge of theft, and he tells the officer who seized him, that if he will go to such a place, and look under such a bush, he will find the stolen goods; or he is charged with murder or assault, and he says he threw the bloody weapon into such a pool, in such a river, and it is there searched for and found; without doubt, these are such strong confirmations of the truth of the confession, as renders it of itself sufficient, if the *corpus* is established *aliunde*, to convict the prisoner'.[1]

1 *Practice* 580.

**5.65**    It must be doubted whether the subsequent development of the 'special knowledge' rule by the Scottish courts is wholly in accordance with Alison's conception. In particular it would appear from the examples which he gives that Alison was probably thinking solely of the situation where the accused tells the police things they do not already know with the corroboration coming from the subsequent finding of the 'real evidence' where the accused said it would be.[1] *Dickson* describes 'real evidence' as 'evidence derived from things'.[2] Under modern conditions a confession can be sufficient evidence for conviction under the 'special knowledge' rule even if it only contains information which was already known to the police and does not bring about the discovery of any 'real evidence' whatsoever.

1 See Sheriff Gordon's commentary to *Wilson and Murray v HM Advocate* 1987 SCCR 217 at 223 and *Walker and Walker* p 440, § 416.
2 Page 991, § 1815.

**5.66** Although the making of a confession is normally sufficiently proved by one witness,[1] where there is nothing to corroborate the confession except 'special knowledge' the making of the confession must be spoken to by at least two witnesses.[2]

1 Para 5.06 above.
2 *Low v HM Advocate* 1993 SCCR 493.

*The first cases*

**5.67** Although *Alison* first expounded the 'special knowledge' rule in 1833, it was to be over a century and a half before the courts had the opportunity to consider the issue. When it did arise, in *Manuel v HM Advocate*,[1] the circumstances could hardly have been more appropriate. As the result of Manuel's confessions to the police, the grave of one of his victims was discovered and one of her shoes was found. Later, as the result of a separate confession, two guns were recovered from the River Clyde. It would have been impossible for anyone other than the perpetrator of the crimes concerned to have known where these items of real evidence were to be found. Lord Justice-General Clyde quoted the passage from *Alison* with approval and commented that it 'might have been written for this case'.

1 1958 JC 41.

**5.68** The earliest reported case showing the typical modern view of 'special knowledge' confessions, and which put paid to any notion that the details in the confession should only be known to the accused or that the confession should result in the finding of previously unknown evidence, was *Smith v HM Advocate*.[1] In this case, which is a fairly routine example of its type, the accused was indicted on 21 charges of housebreaking and convicted of 14. The incriminating evidence against him consisted solely of statements allegedly made to the police. As this decision is the earliest of this particular sequence, it will be considered in some detail.

1 (1978) SCCR Supp 203.

**5.69** The accused was taken to the police station to assist with enquiries into a series of housebreakings and there, in the time-honoured manner, announced 'I want to get the whole thing off my chest'. He was then cautioned and went on to say 'Look, I've done about 20 or 30 houses with that man. I can show you some of them'. There was some dubiety as to whether he was allowed to look at a list of reported housebreakings held by the police, but thereafter he took officers on a guided tour of the houses which he claimed to have broken into and in each case gave an account in 'more or less detail' as to how the job had been done and as to some of the things which had been taken away.

**5.70** A striking feature of this case is the brevity with which the High Court dealt with the issues raised. There is no consideration of authority or principle and, in particular, no consideration of the fact that some, if not all, of the 'knowledge' displayed by Smith was available to the police and that some of this could well have been passed on if Smith was allowed to look at the crime reports. In their Lordships' view:

'It is perfectly clear that a confession can receive corroboration if there is not only proof of the commission of the crime to which it relates but proof aliunde of the truth of the contents of the confession, eg if the confession was made at the time when only the thief or the housebreaker could have known what happened in the various episodes. This is eminently a case in which proof of the contents of the confession was ample or at least sufficient. The fact of the matter is that the confessions were made in circumstances in which the accused had not been charged with any particular crime. They were made at a time when all that the applicant knew was that the police were making enquiries into a series of housebreakings in that area. The particular housebreakings were not identified to the applicant nor did he have at that time any particulars of the articles stolen in the crimes. . . . Now whether or not . . . and it is open to question and was a matter before the jury, he was allowed to glance at the list of reported housebreakings kept in the police office, what is certainly true is that thereafter he took the police in a police car and guided them to the houses . . . . Now in these circumstances, having regard to the way in which this transaction developed there is not the slightest doubt that the evidence of the householders confirming the truth of the contents of the confession, implicating the appellant as the perpetrator of housebreakings which he himself identified to the police, was sufficient to set up the truth of his confessions.'

**5.71** This cannot, with respect, be regarded as a satisfactory consideration of the important issues raised in this case. There is a considerable difference between a confession made at a time when only the perpetrator could have known what happened and the circumstances which existed in the present case. Although the report is brief and includes no details of the evidence or the arguments, it appears that the accused only made some general admissions before he got to the police station. Thereafter it appears that he might have been shown the police list of reported housebreakings before he went out in the police car, which was when the real special knowledge admissions were allegedly made. Surely the possibility of the accused having been influenced (to put it no higher) by the behaviour of the police merits more than the comment that it was 'a matter before the jury'?

**5.72** *Smith* was followed by *Wilson v McAughey*[1] where once again the opinion is brief and lacking in any real consideration of precedent, the sheriff's note being appreciably longer, although at least *Connolly*[2] and *Manuel*[3] do receive an honourable mention. In *Wilson v McAughey* the accused was charged with vandalising a mechanical shovel by starting its engine and driving it into the River Clyde. The machine, which had been parked and secured on dry land, was found submerged in the River Clyde with a broken window and a flat piece of metal in the ignition. When cautioned and charged he replied 'How did you know it was me? I smashed the window of the digger. I put a piece of wire into the key-hole. When I turned it, it started up and started moving. I didn't know how to stop it. I jumped out before it went into the water. I stood and watched it go under the water'.

1 1982 SCCR 398.
2 1958 SLT 79.
3 1958 JC 41.

**5.73** The sheriff relied on *Connolly* and *Manuel* to conclude that there was insufficient corroboration and acquitted the accused on a defence submission of no case to answer. The Crown had proposed an adjustment to the draft-stated case:

'that the perpetrator alone could have known that the windows were sufficiently large through which to climb into the cab; that the machine could not be started with a piece of wire rather than an igition key; that the machine went under the water – not towards, but under the water and that the machine was parked near a "coup" or "rubbish tip"'

but the sheriff refused to accept it because these factors were not exclusively and solely within the knowledge of the accused.

**5.74** On appeal the High Court overturned the acquittal stating:

'The law in the situation here could be summarised in the phrase that the respondent could not have been able to make the statement which he did if he had not been present at the time when the offence libelled had been committed.'

Their Lordships considered that the finding of the broken window, the method of starting, the fact that the machine trundled into the water and the fact that it went under the water all corroborated the accused's incriminating statement, because had he not been present he would not have been able to make reference to these 'very significant factors'.

**5.75** Another point of interest (and concern) in *Wilson v McAughey* is the *dictum* that the confession is corroborated if the accused could not have made it if he 'had not been present at the time when the offence . . . had been committed'. A similar comment was made in *Smith v McPherson*.[1] While these are presumably mere slips of the judicial tongue and it may be unfair to take such remarks out of context, this does point to one of the main potential dangers of the situation, the possibility of detailed 'special knowledge' being available to someone who had seen the crime, but was not himself the actual offender.

1 1983, unreported, CO Circular A5/83.

**5.76** Several subsequent cases have shown just how little evidence is necessary to justify the application of the 'special knowledge' tag. Thus in *Annan v Bain*[1] a statement 'It's a fair cop, we stole the white car' was held to show 'special knowledge' since nothing had been said by the police to indicate that they were interested in the theft of any car, never mind a white one.

1 1986 SCCR 60.

**5.77** Likewise in *MacDonald v HM Advocate*[1] when the accused was cautioned and charged with robbery he said 'I've already told you that I did that one with Kenny and Bruce'. He was tried along with two co-accused called Kenneth Ross and Bruce Murray and all were convicted. On appeal it was held that the appellant's knowledge of the involvement of his co-accused amounted to special knowledge sufficient to provide corroboration. It is probably idle to speculate on what would have happened if the jury had acquitted the co-accused but convicted MacDonald. Presumably the conviction would have had to be quashed since the facts necessary for the proof of special knowledge would not have been established. Even more intriguing is the question of what would have happened if only one of the co-accused had been convicted. MacDonald's conviction could probably have been upheld on the ratio of *Gilmour v HM Advocate*[2] but is is respectfully submitted that the bare naming of accomplices with no verifiable details of what part they played, or anything else to confirm the reliability of the confession, stretches the concept of corroboration to breaking point.

1  1987 SCCR 581.
2  1983 SLT 16; para 5.81 below.

**5.78**  In *Bainbridge v Scott*[1] the accused was charged with vandalising two motor vehicles and 'special knowledge' was found in his awareness that the first vehicle was a car and the second a van.

1  1988 SLT 871.

**5.79**  Probably the most extreme application of the 'special knowledge' principle to date is *Hutchison v Valentine*[1] where the accused was convicted of breaking into a hotel room and stealing a television set which had been recovered abandoned in a car park. When interviewed by the police he was simply told that a room in the hotel had been broken into. He then informed them, 'I done it on my ain. I canna really mind where aboot in the hotel I got it. I was drunk. I dumped it'. The High Court held that the references to 'it' and 'dumped' showed that the accused was aware that the crime involved a single piece of property which had subsequently been left somewhere by the thief rather than being carried off.

1  1990 SCCR 569.

**5.80**  Finally, *Moran v HM Advocate*[1] stands as a warning to accused persons to check their information before trying to be too clever. Moran had been in police custody for an unconnected matter when he offered to give the police information relating to a murder. He then made a detailed statement containing considerable circumstantial information about the crime which he claimed he had learned from one Morrison. Unfortunately, Morrison had been in no position to commit the murder since he had been in custody himself at the material time and the Crown successfully founded on Moran's statement as showing 'special knowledge' of the murder.

1  1990 SCCR 40.

*Statements partly consistent and partly inconsistent*

**5.81**  *Gilmour v HM Advocate*[1] is particularly important as the first authority on the question of a statement containing admissions which are partly consistent and partly inconsistent with the facts. Gilmour, who was charged with rape and murder, had made two confessions to the police admitting killing the victim, but which differed from the known facts in several important details. One of the senior police officers involved in the case was of the view that the first statement, which embraced the drawing of a sketch of the locus, contained so many discrepancies that it did not form a basis for cautioning and charging Gilmour and he ordered his release from custody. The second statement was essentially a repetition of the first made to different police officers. The discrepancies were undoubtedly substantial and were, naturally, fully exploited by defence counsel, and the trial judge himself observed that the corroborative sources were few. Regrettably the report does not specify fully what the discrepancies were and the trial judge did not go into them in detail, but even some of the matters which the trial judge regarded as points of similarity contained much that was in fact inconsistent, particularly Gilmour's claim to have hit the victim several times on the head with a branch which was inconsistent with the medical evidence.

**1** 1983 SLT 16.

**5.82** After rehearsing the points of similarity, the trial judge directed the jury:

'Now these ladies and gentlemen are the details which you might think corroborate the statement, if you ever reach the stage of accepting it as a voluntary statement and believing it to be true. And as for the discrepancies, you must consider whether these discrepancies and the discrepancies in what he said [in the first statement] were due to the statement being fabricated, that is made up, or whether they are due to the fact that the accused was the murderer but that he was in such a state of panic, having been caught unawares by a young girl who found him masturbating by the side of the path, that he didn't know how far from the path they ended up, he didn't know how far they had travelled, and he didn't know what he used to strangle the girl.'

**5.83** On appeal, the trial judge's decision to rehearse the points of identity and not the points of discrepancy was criticised by defence counsel. However, the High Court did not agree: 'In our opinion that was not a valid criticism. It is not the function of the judge to rehearse every piece of evidence in his charge to the jury which in our procedure does not call for a review of all the evidence'.

**5.84** Their Lordships then set out how the trial court should approach the matter:

'When looking for points of corroboration attention has to be focussed on those parts of the evidence which are said to provide that corroboration. If there is an absence of a point or points which have a significance then the jury can take these into account when deciding whether or not the points of proffered corroboration should be accepted, and, if accepted, what weight should be attached to them . . . Once [the statements] were accepted, the crucial question was whether the points of identity were sufficiently satisfactory in the jury's mind to constitute the required corroboration. It was to these matters that the judge gave detailed and individual attention. In our opinion that was a line to take which in the circumstances cannot be faulted'.

**5.85** The High Court went on to make it clear that there was no question of anything as crude as numerical superiority entering into consideration:

'The argument seemed to be that as there were more points of discrepancy than there were of identity the jury could not reasonably proceed on the points of identity. Counsel started off by talking of balance . . . but eventually conceded that this was not the proper approach. Manifestly it is not a matter of a numerical mathematical equation or balance. Where a statement contains points of identity and points of discrepancy, then, as previously indicated, it is for the jury to decide whether they are going to accept and proceed upon the points of identity, and if they do so the only question then is whether these points are sufficient in law to constitute corroboration of the admission of guilt. In the instant case the points of identity, if accepted, were clearly sufficient in law, and the judge very properly left the issue to the jury. The verdict indicates how the jury responded.'

**5.86** Thus, the position is that where there are both consistencies and inconsistencies between the confession and facts, the jury has to decide whether it is satisfied that the confession is sufficiently corroborated. This assumes, of course, that the consistencies are in themselves sufficient to provide corroboration, although, if they are not, the case will presumably fall on a submission of no case to answer and never reach the jury.

*Confessions containing details widely known*

**5.87** The cases previously discussed show how far and how rapidly the concept of 'special knowledge' had departed from the notion that the information contained in the confession should only be known to the perpetrator of the crime. However, in all the cases the information given, although not exclusively within the knowledge of the perpetrator, could be described as being of limited circulation, in the sense that, apart from the perpetrator, it was only known to the police and a few individuals directly affected by the crimes, However, it was inevitable that the High Court would sooner or later have to deal with the question of a confession containing details which had become widely known.

**5.88**   The first hint of the High Court's likely view came in *McAvoy v HM Advocate*[1] where 'special knowledge' was only one of several issues raised and the case rather stands apart from the main line of cases on the subject. However, Lord Hunter made an important observation on the weight of evidence when he said:

'I would only add that it is not, in my opinion, necessarily fatal to the ratio of [*Connolly* and *Manuel*] that persons other than the accused had become aware of the facts and circumstances used as corroboration before the confession itself had been made. This however does not mean to say that passage of time between the date of the crime and the date of a detailed confession is of no moment, since such a delay might in some circumstances make it more likely that an accused person had acquired his knowledge of detail not as a perpetrator of the crime or offence but as a recipient of information from other sources.'

1   1983 SLT 16.

**5.89**   The first, and so far the only, case to deal squarely with the issue is *Wilson and Murray v HM Advocate*.[1] This case related to the attempted rape and brutal murder of the half-sister of the accused Murray whose naked body had been found at the bottom of a steep slope below a footpath. There were no immediate suspects and police inquiries, although intensive, were initially unsuccessful. Many people, including the two accused, were interviewed, house-to-house inquiries were made and at one point the assistance of the local radio station, Radio Clyde, was obtained. In the course of the broadcast it was disclosed that the victim had been strangled with her own brassiere.

1   1987 SCCR 217.

**5.90**   The murder had taken place on 22 May 1986 and on 15 June Murray was taken to Drumchapel police office in connection with an unrelated matter. Quite by coincidence, around the time that Murray was taken to Drumchapel, Wilson went voluntarily to Clydebank police station to discuss his earlier statement. (The police knew that he and Murray had been in the area around the material time). Both of them, quite independently, and in separate police stations then proceeded to make confessions each of which was, according to the Lord Justice-General, 'a detailed confession of guilt of the murder which, subject to quite insignificant differences of detail, was identical [with the other]'.

**5.91**   The story which emerged was that the accused had been in the woods engaging in a homosexual act together when the victim happened on the scene and saw what was going on. They were terrified that she would report the matter to her parents, and, as the Lord Justice-General put it, 'proceeded to make sure that she would be unable to do that'. The details of the statements tallied closely with what had been found at the scene of the crime particularly in regard to the position of the deceased's anorak and Murray also drew a sketch of the position of the body. Apart from the confessions there was no incriminating evidence against either accused and, as Sheriff Gordon points out in his commentary, some of the most striking details of the confessions were not capable of being corroborated by independent evidence of their accuracy. The trial judge charged the jury as follows:

'[I]n order to corroborate a so-called self-corroborating confession it is not necessary to prove that only the perpetrator of the crime could have known all the details in the confession. It is for the jury to decide if the only reasonable explanation of the accused's knowledge of these details is that he was the perpetrator. Now it is sufficient to provide the necessary corroboration that the accused gave evidence in his confession of knowledge of details which otherwise he had no reason to be aware of. The question therefore for the jury is really this: do these confessions . . . convince you that, quite apart from the account given by the accused, they must have been there at the perpetration of the crime in order to give that account? . . . [I]t is entirely for you to say whether you think, if these statements are accepted as having been given, could these accused have given these statements unless they had been there and had known what the details of the crime were. That is the test and you will have to apply your minds to that if you get to that stage.'

**5.92** On appeal it was conceded that this direction could not be criticised, but it was argued that having regard to the widespread knowledge of the details of the murder the case should not have been allowed to go to the jury. In dismissing the appeal the Lord Justice-General quoted with approval Lord Hunter's *dictum* in *McAvoy* and went on:

'In our opinion the trial judge would not have been entitled in this case to sustain a motion that there was no case to answer. There was in law quite sufficient evidence capable of providing corroboration of these remarkable, almost identical confessions made by each appellant in separate police stations . . . . Each provided an identical and powerful motive for the dreadful crime, and was redolent of having been made by someone who had been present when the crime was committed. The evidence of the coincidence between the details of the killing which each confession disclosed, and what was found after the event, was sufficient in law for corroborative purposes if the jury were prepared to find that the accurate knowledge of the crime revealed in the statements of each appellant was his own knowledge as one of the perpetrators. It was not for the trial judge to evaluate the weight which should be given to the circumstance that by 15th June 1986 many people knew or had heard of many of the details of the crime. That was essentially a matter for the jury to consider under the proper directions which were given and that, indeed, is precisely what Lord Hunter had in mind when he said what he did in *McAvoy*.'

It may be remarked in passing that the trial judge apparently did not direct the jury that Wilson's statement was not evidence against Murray and *vice versa*. Although, in fairness, this point did not form one of the grounds of appeal it is surprising that it was not mentioned by the High Court, and the Lord Justice-General did, at least to a point, appear to regard the similarties of the statements as a matter of some importance. This harks back to the misstatement of the law in *Annan v Bain and Hamill*.[1] The proper view, that a statement made by accused A outwith the presence of accused B is not evidence against B, has now been clearly restated in *Buchan v HM Advocate*.[2]

1 1986 SCCR 60; para 3.04 above.
2 1993 SCCR 1076.

*'Special knowledge' not established*

**5.93**    The reports contain few examples of the High Court being prepared to overturn convictions based on 'special knowledge' confessions no matter how tenuous the corroboration.

**5.94**    In *Walker v Smith*[1] the accused had made an unequivocal admission to an unsuccessful attempt to break into a school. Three panes of glass had been broken in a door and one of the two bolts securing it had been withdrawn, the other still being in place. The accused told the police that he had been disturbed and at his trial the sheriff took the view that the partial unbolting of the door showed that the would-be housebreaker was disturbed. Since there was no evidence from the janitor or anyone else that they had disturbed the accused, the High Court had little difficulty in overturning the conviction and pointing out that the condition of the door was 'utterly neutral'.

1 1975 SLT (Notes) 85.

**5.95**    In *Woodland v Hamilton*,[1] a decision very much on its own facts, the accused was charged along with a man called Halliday with breaking into a house and stealing a number of items including a videorecorder. When interviewed under caution by the police he said 'Aye, Johnny Halliday told me you got him and that he said he told the truth so I'll be honest and tell you. The video went to Kevin Boyle. The suitcase was dumped. It's the only housebreaking I've ever done'. There was a second admission following caution and charge but it was a simple confession. The sheriff found as a fact that the police had not mentioned Boyle's name to the accused before he made this statement. At the trial Boyle admitted having been in possession of the video but denied that he had obtained it from the accused. The sheriff was clearly less than impressed with his evidence but convicted Woodland on the basis that his admission was corroborated by the fact that Boyle was the resetter of the video-recorder. Halliday was acquitted.

1 1990 SCCR 166.

**5.96** Rather surprisingly the High Court overturned the conviction. Their Lordships accepted that the test to be applied was whether the only reasonable explanation of the accused's knowledge was the fact that he was the perpetrator. However, the reference to Boyle as the resetter came after a sentence in which the accused said he had been in conversation with Halliday and that Halliday had given him at least some information:

'It is therefore possible that the appellant may have obtained the name of Boyle from Halliday. Had there been evidence from Halliday to the effect that he had given no such information to the appellant then it might well be said that the only reasonable explanation of the appellant's knowledge was that he was the perpetrator. As it is however the appellant could have become aware of Boyle's involvement even though he himself was not the perpetrator of the crime. This is particularly so having regard to the lapse of nearly eleven months between the date of the crime and the date of the confession.'

**5.97** In an *obiter* comment in *Low v HM Advocate*[1] the High Court expressed 'considerable doubt' as to whether the statement 'He was lying on the ground in a pool of blood' could be held to disclose special knowledge.

1 1993 SCCR 493 at 509E.

*Some observations*

**5.98** The modern application of the 'special knowledge' principle has attracted criticism from commentators both within and outside Scotland. The general thrust of the criticism is that the present situation gives insufficient weight to the protection of the accused.

**5.99** The present writer would respectfully associate himself with Sheriff Gordon's argument that the 'special knowledge' rule should be restricted to facts unknown to the police. As Sheriff Gordon has pointed out, it is:

'a little misleading to say that a person cannot be convicted of a crime in Scotland on the basis only of a confession made by him to the police. He can be virtually so convicted, providing only that the confession is sufficiently detailed to satisfy a jury that it is reliable, and provided that the fact that the crime was committed by someone is independently proved.'[1]

1 Commentary to *Wilson and Murray v HM Advocate* 1987 SCCR 217 at 223.

**5.100**    The existing state of the law means that any police officer, possibly under pressure to solve a major crime, who is prepared to fabricate a confession or 'touch up' a genuine one to make it more convincing, has no need even to look beyond the existing state of police knowledge since it has long ceased to be a requirement of the law that the 'special knowledge' should be something unknown to the police. Indeed, since Sheriff Gordon wrote the passage quoted above, decisions like *MacDonald v HM Advocate*[1] and *Hutchison v Valentine*[2] have diminished almost to vanishing point the amount of detail which the courts require before a confession is held to show 'special knowledge'. Any police officer who is considering engaging in malpractice in relation to confession evidence is hardly likely to be deterred by a judicial decision which holds that 'I dumped it' is 'special knowledge' of the details of a theft by housebreaking.

1 1987 SCCR 581; para 5.77 above.
2 1990 SCCR 569; para 5.79 above.

**5.101**    The *obiter* observation in *Low v HM Advocate* that 'he was lying on the ground in a pool of blood' is unlikely to disclose special knowledge is, with respect, both welcome and overdue and it is to be hoped that it represents the beginning of a reappraisal of the current state of the law.

**5.102**    Even if there is no deliberate malpractice, there are other dangers, as one perceptive English commentator has noted:

'Accurate details do not always mean a confession is genuine. Therein lies the difficulty with the Scottish approach . . . Convincing details may be found in a confession through coincidence, because the information was in the public domain, because of contact with the real criminal or a lesser degree of criminality than that confessed to and/or deliberate police assistance with the composition of the statement or unconscious transmission of information to the suspect during questioning by leading questions and dissatisfaction with answers . . . As it stands the Scottish corroboration rule does not preclude conviction on a false confession and may too readily allay appellate court and jury doubts about the accused's guilt.'[1]

1 R Pattenden 'Should Confessions be Corroborated?' (1991) 107 LQR 317 at 336. Similar views were expressed by native Scots in (1989) 158 SCOLAG 168 and (1989) 34 JLSS 448.

**5.103**  While police interviewing techniques have been the subject of several studies in England, there is a striking absence of Scottish research into this important area and in the absence of independent research one must remain uncertain as to what goes on in Scottish police stations. All that can be said is that the Scottish case reports do not contain any recent example of a conviction being quashed because it has been established that there has been police malpractice in relation to confession evidence. In addition, the much shorter time during which a Scottish suspect can find himself in police hands probably also diminishes the risks to him.

**5.104**  Nevertheless, one common thread running through the cases discussed in this chapter is a largely uncritical assumption by the judiciary of police veracity and objectivity. Lord Robertson's observation in *Gilmour v HM Advocate*[1] that it was a 'knife edge case, so there is a motive for the police putting in additional statements like this' is one of the few reported judicial acknowledgments of the possibility of police malpractice. Experience in other jurisdictions has shown what can happen when the trust placed in the police is abused. Several of the major English miscarriages of justice have involved confession evidence to a greater or lessor extent. Probably the best known are Timothy Evans,[2] the 'Confait' case,[3] the 'Guildford Four',[4] the 'Birmingham Six'[5] and Winston Silcott.[6] While there are no reported examples of such abominations in Scotland, and modern developments, particularly tape-recording, have increased the protection of the accused, the current state of the law allows no scope for complacency.

1  1982 SCCR 590 at 603.
2  See generally L Kennedy *Ten Rillington Place*.
3  See generally C Price and J Caplan *The Confait Confessions*.
4  The Times, 20 October 1989.
5  *McIlkenney v R* (1991) 93 Crim App Rep 287.
6  The Times, 26 November 1991.

# 6. The record of the extra-judicial confession

## INTRODUCTION

**6.01**  One of the major problems inherent in confession evidence is the question of the accuracy of the record of an extra-judicial confession. Many of the difficulties stem from the fact that the majority of extra-judicial confessions are made in police stations or in other situations where only the accused and the police are present and either side may have an interest in telling something other than the whole truth. This chapter is concerned with the means which may be adopted to serve the triple purposes of protecting the interests of the suspect, protecting the police from false allegations, and providing an accurate record of what took place to assist the courts to reach the best possible decision on the issues of admissibility and sufficiency discussed in the previous chapters.

**6.02**  Confession evidence attracts a very high status in the eyes of the Scottish courts, but, as has already been pointed out, it would be all too easy for an unscrupulous police officer to fabricate a false confession or 'touch up' a genuine one to make it more convincing, for example by adding in some 'special knowledge'. Dickson's views on this point are particularly striking.[1] On the other hand, the accused has an obvious interest in denying what he is alleged to have said; oral evidence of what took place between the accused and the police is often fiercely disputed and such disputes, apart from using up scarce court time, may involve quite unwarranted attacks on the integrity of the policemen concerned. Matters such as accent, tone of voice or the context in which certain things were said may also be of importance in deciding the admissibility or sufficiency of a confession. Mendacity apart, the possibility of an honest mistake or a lapse of memory cannot be discounted, problems which are, of course, by no means exclusive to confession evidence. However, one important feature of confession evidence has been put thus:

'It is normally acquired by officials aware, at the time they acquire it, that it is very likely to be presented before a court. It is possible for these officials to take steps to ensure that the record is both accurate and reliable and [it is] possible for the law to require or encourage them to take such steps.'[2]

It is probably self-evident that an accurate record of what transpired between the accused and the police will assist in determining whether the accused confessed at all, and, if so, under what circumstances and in what terms. In other words an accurate record will materially assist a court in deciding the difficult issues of fact and law to which confession evidence so often gives rise.

1 *The Law of Evidence in Scotland* pp 261–262, §§ 377 and 378.
2 Mirfield *Confessions* p 3.

## WRITTEN STATEMENTS

**6.03**  Traditionally, Scots law has relied for proof of the accused's words on oral evidence from police officers, frequently using their notebooks as *aides-memoire*. In Scots law a police officer's notebook, unless lodged as a production in its own right, is confidential to the officer, the defence only being entitled to see the notes if the officer produces or refers to the notebook in the course of giving his evidence.[1]

1 *Hinshelwood v Auld* 1926 JC 4; see further para 6.09 ff below.

**6.04**  Written statements by accused persons are extremely rare, apart from post-charge 'voluntary statements'. In current practice an accused's post-charge statement will be reduced to writing either by the accused himself or, much more commonly, by two officers unconnected with the case, and signed by the accused. It will contain an acknowledgment of the caution and the offer of legal advice and a statement that the accused has either read over the statement or had it read over to him. The signed statement will then be lodged as a production and spoken to by the officers who took it. The origins of this practice are uncertain, although it was probably derived from the declaration. It may also be that the modern Scottish practice was at least partly influenced by the Judges' Rules in England, but in any event it is now of such universal application that it can be regarded as being beyond challenge and has been approved by judicial comment.[1] On the other hand there is no reported case where evidence of a post-charge statement has been held inadmissible because the normal practice was not followed.

1 *Tonge v HM Advocate* 1982 SCCR 313 at 350. See also para 2.92 above.

**6.05** There are only two Scottish cases dealing with this issue. Firstly, *Hamilton v HM Advocate*[1] is against the idea of the written statement being anything more than a simple written record of what the accused said. It had been argued that where the Crown *per incuriam* failed to produce the written statement, the oral evidence of the police officers as to what the accused had said was inadmissible as not being the 'best evidence'. This argument received short shrift from Lord Justice-Clerk Wheatley:

'This submission proceeds on a misconception. When the statement was made it was made orally to the interviewing officers. Their appraisement of the statement was what they individually heard. What was said by the applicant was then committed to writing by one of them and eventually read over to the applicant and signed by him as correct. But what the officers heard was primary not secondary evidence. The different methods by which the officers could speak to what was said by the applicant at the time attach to the reliability and not to the competency of the evidence. Committing the statement to writing and getting an accused to sign it as accurate may forestall a challenge to the accuracy of what is recorded as having been said by him, but that does not render incompetent the possibly more vulnerable recollection of what was actually said.'

1  1980 JC 66.

**6.06** Secondly, *Cordiner v HM Advocate*[1] is clear authority for the proposition that the normal practice is simply practice and not rules of law and a voluntary statement does not become inadmissible merely because it was not taken by an independent officer. In this case the accused had asked to speak with one of the investigating policemen who went on to record his voluntary statement. Such a departure from normal practice simply becomes an aspect of fairness.[2] *Cordiner* can also be regarded as authority for the proposition that where the voluntary statement has been both tape-recorded and hand written, it is unnecessary to produce the handwritten statement as well as the tape.

1  1991 SCCR 652.
2  Cf *Rodgers v Hamilton* 1993 GWD 30–1863.

**6.07** Although a written and signed statement is much more difficult to challenge than a policeman's simple oral evidence, a point acknowledged by Lord Wheatley, such methods of recording confessions have their limitations. As already noted, there has been virtually no research into Scottish police interviewing and in the absence of research one must remain uncertain as to what happens in Scottish police stations, particularly as, in Lord Devlin's words, 'it is the general habit of the police never to admit the slightest departure from correctness'.[1] However, the Thomson Committee was clearly unhappy:

'An unfortunate result of the present state of the law is that the police may be tempted to take answers given to questioning over a period, put them together into a single statement, and present that to the court as a spontaneous voluntary statement. Some of us with experience of these matters have seen so-called voluntary statements which covered so precisely the disparate points of the police case as to make their spontaneity highly suspect. But in disputes in court as to the circumstances in which a statement was made it is difficult, if not impossible, for a judge to reject the statement as inadmissible on the grounds that the police account of the circumstances is untrue.'[2]

1 *The Criminal Prosecution in England* p 39.
2 Departmental Committee on Criminal Procedure in Scotland (Second Report) (1975, Cmnd 6218) para 7.11.

**6.08** Another colourful observation from Lord Devlin was also approved by the Thomson Committee:

'Lawyer-like tendencies flourish to an even greater extent among the police than they do at the bar or on the Bench. The police have sometimes seemed to treat the [English] Judges' Rules as if they were a drill manual and to be unwilling to admit the slightest deviation from the text. Rather than become engaged in a discussion about whether a question was or was not necessary to remove an ambiguity, some police witnesses seem to have preferred stoutly to deny that they asked any questions at all and even to maintain that they hardly opened their mouths. Consequently statements have sometimes been put in evidence which have been said to be the prisoner's own unaided work as taken down by the police officer and in which the prisoner has recounted in the stately language of the police station (where, for example, people never eat but partake of refreshment and never quarrel but indulge in altercations) the tale of his misdeeds.'[1]

Many of these problems are now being eliminated with the introduction of tape-recording. However, there is no legal requirement on the police to tape-record and the existing law, such as it is, will continue to be relevant in cases where there has been no recording.

1 *The Criminal Prosecution in England* p 39.

## NOTES AND NOTEBOOKS

**6.09** As previously mentioned, Scots law has generally proceeded on the basis that the primary evidence of what the accused said is the oral evidence of the police officer who heard it, and Scots law has never accorded any special legal status to written statements or notes of interviews. This is consistent with the law's general reluctance to require the police to record information in a particular way as a condition of admissibility except in the unusual situation where it is necessary for the information to be recorded in a particular way so that, for example, its accuracy can be verified.[1]

1 *Cummings v HM Advocate* 1982 SCCR 108; *Forbes v HM Advocate* 1990 SCCR 69.

**6.10** In the case of notes in a police officer's notebook, there is, compared to England, a notable lack of case law, but the accepted view is that such notes merely become part of the officer's oral testimony.[1] While a written, signed statement will normally be lodged as a production, it is generally not the practice to lodge a policeman's notebook, although there is no reason why, in an approriate case, this should not be done.[2] Apart from such unusual situations, the

'familiar practice in both solemn and summary procedure is that the policeman's notebook is not lodged, he is allowed to refer to any entry which he made contemporaneously with the events to which he is speaking, and the defence advocate may inspect the entry if he wishes to do so.'[3]

1 Walker and Walker *The Law of Evidence in Scotland* p 363, § 341(b).
2 Macphail *Evidence* para 8.47, § 8.47.
3 *Macphail* para 8.47.

**6.11** It does not appear to be normal practice in Scotland for the accused to be shown, far less asked to sign, notes in a policeman's notebook, and although officers are frequently asked in court whether the note was made at the time, and generally reply in the affirmative, the issue is rarely explored in depth. It would, in any event, be extremely difficult to prove otherwise and there would not appear to be any reported Scottish case in which a police officer has been refused permission to refresh his memory from his notes because they were not made at the time. The rule requiring notes to be made at the time is generally applied on the common-sense basis that the notes should have been made as soon as practicable after the making of the statement but again there are no cases. In England the Court of Appeal has held that

'. . . a witness may refresh his memory by reference to any writing made or verified by himself concerning, and contemporaneously with, the facts to which he testifies. "Contemporaneously" is a somewhat misleading word in the context of the memory refreshing rule. It is sufficient for the purposes of the rule, if the writing was made or verified at a time when the facts were still fresh in the witness's memory.'[1]

1 *Attorney General's Reference (No 3 of 1979)* (1979) 69 Crim App Rep 411.

**6.12** In Scottish practice it is by no means unknown for one police officer simply to check and sign the notes in his colleague's notebook, a practice which does not appear to have attracted any reported judicial disapproval and which is consistent with the English *dictum* just quoted. Similarly, there has been no reported judicial disapproval of the practice of one officer copying notes from a colleague's notebook.

**6.13** Before tape-recording intervened, Scottish procedure in relation to the recording of interviews with suspects was still in a comparatively undeveloped state, a fact which was probably a function of Scots law's historic attachment to *viva voce* evidence. The position was broadly similar to the pre-PACE situation in England and subject to the same criticisms.[1] Verbatim contemporaneous records, although not unknown, were rare, preparation of notes after the event was the rule rather than the exception, suspects seldom saw what went into the notebook, and falsification was difficult, if not impossible, to establish in court. There was (and still is) a total absence of any enforceable legal requirement that record of interviews be kept in any particular format, or indeed that interviews be recorded at all.

1 See Mirfield *Confessions* pp 6–13; G Williams 'The Authentication of Statements to the Police' [1979] Crim LR 6, especially pp 11–12.

## RECORDING BY TAPE AND VIDEO

### Introduction and early history

**6.14** Nowadays it may seem self-evident that a tape-recording, or possibly a video-recording, of what took place between the police and the suspect will offer standards of accuracy and completeness which cannot be matched by any form of written record. Even verbatim contemporaneous noting cannot compete since the tone or inflexion of the suspect's voice cannot be captured on paper. English experience also showed that the requirement to take such notes tended to interrupt the flow of the interview and possibly deprived the police of an important psychological advantage. It has been suggested that the problems of verbatim contemporaneous noting may have been one reason why the English police latterly modified their previously implacable hostility to the tape-recording of interviews.[1]

1 J Baldwin 'Police Interviews on Tape' [1990] New LJ 662.

**6.15** Tentative steps towards the recording of police interviews were being taken in America in the 1940s. It may be that the Americans harboured fewer illusions about the capacity of their police to indulge in questionable and occasionally downright illegal practices and as early as 1942 rule 505 of the American Law Institute's Model Code of Evidence commented:

'In some instances confessions taken by the police have been recorded by a sound film. To impose a requirement on the police that they should take no confession unless recorded is believed to be practicable, effective and desireable . . . Certainly wherever it is practicable to supply and use the necessary equipment in a reasonably efficient manner it should be done and the courts should encourage such procedure in any legitimate manner.'

It is also noteworthy that there is a reported American example of the filming of an interview as early as 1948.[1]

1 *People v Dabb* (1948) 32 Cal 2d 491.

**6.16** The idea that recordings might play a part in the police investigation seems to have crossed the Atlantic in the early 1950s,[1] and by the late 1950s the idea of tape-recording had been enthusiastically embraced by Glanville Williams who suggested that as well as recording confessions, the police might tape witness statements, and he also advocated the use by the police of pocket tape-recorders.[2]

1 T R Radley 'Recording as Testimony to the Truth' [1954] Crim LR 96.
2 (1957–58) 4 JSPTL (NS) 217 at 226; [1959] Crim LR 313 at 314. See also [1960] Crim LR 325 at 342.

**6.17** Although taping of police interviews was still a long way off, by the early 1960s the courts were beginning to have some experience of the evidential use of tape-recording in other contexts and although there were difficulties, notably in the use of transcripts, the tapes themselves were generally admitted in evidence.[1]

1 For the earlier English decisions see R E Auld 'The Admissibility of Tape Recordings in Criminal Proceedings: A Comparative Note' [1961] Crim LR 598.

**6.18** The first, and for many years the only, Scottish case involving a tape was *Hopes and Lavery v HM Advocate*[1] in which a blackmail victim was fitted with a concealed microphone and transmitter prior to meeting the blackmailer in Glasgow Central Station. Police officers in a room in the station had a receiver, loudspeaker and tape-recorder and other officers were able to watch the conversation take place although they could not hear it. The conversation was transmitted from the microphone to the receiver, to the loudspeaker and ultimately to the tape-recorder. At the trial, evidence was led from a police officer who heard the conversation coming over the loudspeaker. The tape-recording was indistinct and, as might be expected, contained a lot of extraneous noise, so in order to provide an intelligible account of the conversation, the tape was played over several times to a stenographer who made a shorthand record of what she heard and then prepared a transcript, which Lord Justice-General Clyde later described as 'really more in the nature of a reconstruction by her of what the conversation, in her view, must have been'. The evidence of the stenographer and her transcript was, with considerable hesitation, held admissible. However, the High Court made it clear that, in the future, evidence on the interpretation of tape-recordings should, if possible, be given by persons who had expert qualifications.

1   1960 JC 104.

**6.19**   The most important decision of the period in England was *R v Maqsud Ali, R v Ashif Hussain*[1] where the English Court of Criminal Appeal considered *Hopes and Lavery* and took the point that there was no difference in principle between a tape-recording and a photograph. Although their Lordships declined to lay down an exhaustive set of rules, they did hold that a tape-recording was admissible provided its accuracy could be proved, the voices properly identified and the evidence was otherwise relevant and admissible.

1   [1965] 2 All ER 464.

**6.20**   In Scotland the tape-recording of police interviews was first discussed by the Thomson Committee[1] which recommended that the interrogation of suspects in police stations should be recorded on tape 'in order to provide a safeguard for persons being interrogated in the privacy of a police station and also to protect the police against unjustified allegations'. The Committee also recommended that voluntary statements should be tape-recorded. It is noteworthy that the Committee considered that no account of an unrecorded interrogation should be admissible, even where this had resulted from failure of the equipment. Opinions will doubtless differ on whether the subsequent failure to give effect to this recommendation was a good thing.

1   Second Report para 7.23.

**6.21**   The Thomson Committee did not concern itself particularly with feasibility, although it did carry out a small practical experiment which proved technically satisfactory, and it noted that both the availability of more sophisticated equipment and better training for police officers would improve matters even further. Tampering with tapes was considered unlikely, but to reduce the possibility the tape was to be sealed and placed in the custody of the procurator fiscal as soon as possible after the interrogation.

**6.22** A research study into the tape-recording of police interviews with suspects began in May 1980 with the establishment of experimental schemes in Dundee and Falkirk; later the experiment was extended to Aberdeen and Glasgow. Monitoring was undertaken between the date of inception of the experiment and 31 December 1983. Tape-recording was initially restricted to CID investigations in cases which were thought by the police to justify prosecution in the sheriff or High Court and where the suspect was aged 16 or over.[1]

1 The guidelines to be followed, which were revised in 1982, are set out in full in E C M Wozniak 'The Tape Recording of Police Interviews with Suspected Persons in Scotland' (SHHD 1985) p 131 ff.

**6.23** An interim research report was produced covering the first 24 months of the experiment and as the first UK study of tape-recording of police interrogations it naturally attracted some interest.[1] This early research indicated that only a minimal number of suspects refused to be taped and even fewer attempted to fake maltreatment or assault by the police. However, as far as the behaviour of the police was concerned, the figures showed that there had been a dramatic effect on both the length and the content of interviews. There was a dramatic rise, particularly in Falkirk, of suspects who made statements before arriving at the police station, and there were delays between the suspect arriving at the police station and the tape-recorder being activated.[2]

1 'Tape Recording of Police Interviews: Interim Report – The First 24 Months' (SHHD, 1982).
2 M McConville and P Morrell 'Recording the Interrogation: Have The Police Got It Taped?' [1983] Crim LR 158.

**6.24** That tape-recording, particularly in Dundee, got off to a shaky start was due in no small measure to the decision by Lord Jauncey in *HM Advocate v McFadden*[1] where a whole interview was held inadmissible on the grounds of cross-examination, even though parts of it were held to be entirely fair to the accused. It was to be some three years before the issue was settled and *McFadden* overruled by *Lord Advocate's Reference (No 1 of 1983).*[2]

1 August 1980, unreported; see 1983 SCCR 208.
2 1984 SCCR 62.

**6.25** The working group set up to monitor the experiment reported in 1985 and at the same time published the full results of the monitoring exercise.[1] The research evidence showed that tape-recording had had a substantial effect on the way the police both prepared for and carried out interviews. By the time the full picture was known, the police in Dundee had settled down to be perhaps the most scrupulous of the four groups of officers in complying with the requirements of the scheme and they were beginning to come to the view that once they had adjusted to it it was possible to operate tape-recording successfully and with a minimum of inconvenience, a view which was also, to a lesser extent, held in Aberdeen. However, officers in Falkirk and Glasgow remained suspicious of tape-recording and admitted to devices to avoid it.[2] While it has to be borne in mind that the bulk of the research was carried out before *McFadden* was overruled, the tenor of the evidence gathered showed that the police, while acknowledging the potential for reducing attacks on their credibility, were generally hostile to tape-recording and the most favourable response to its extension was likely to be grudging acceptance.

1  See articles by J MacLean in (1986) 112 SCOLAG 9 and (1986) 113 SCOLAG 21.
2  Wozniak, para 6.22, above, p 17.

**6.26**  Nevertheless, the working group took the view that the experiment had proved the technical feasibility of tape-recording and the debate had reached the stage where the introduction of a national scheme was inevitable. The ultimate objective was seen as the tape-recording of all interviews in police stations, but having regard to the practical and financial problems involved, it was recommended that the categories of interviews to be taped should remain as they had been during the experiment. Introduction throughout Scotland should be phased on a geographical basis and national guidelines should be drawn up, although legislation was not considered necessary.

**6.27**  Following a period of consultation, the Secretary of State for Scotland announced in a written answer to Parliament on 6 April 1987 that he was asking chief constables throughout Scotland to begin the necessary preliminary work on buildings, equipment and training with a view to a rolling programme of implementation beginning on 1 April 1988. The Secretary of State also announced that suspects under the age of 16 were to be brought within the scope of tape-recording.

## The Scottish tape-recording scheme

**6.28**  Apart from the inclusion of suspects under 16, the tape-recording scheme as introduced differed little from the experimental one. Tape-recording currently only applies to CID interviews in a police station, where the offence is deemed serious enough to warrant prosecution in the High Court or sheriff court (and the stipendiary magistrate's court in Glasgow). Three categories of persons are to be tape-recorded: (a) those who have signed voluntary attendance forms; (b) those who have been detained under section 2 of the Criminal Justice (Scotland) Act 1980; and (c) those who have been arrested. An accused person who is in custody for one offence may be interviewed in the course of investigation of others for which he is a suspect.

**6.29** Tape-recording has had no effect on the rules of admissibility and the overriding requirement of fairness is maintained. If there is any doubt about whether tape-recording is appropriate, the requirement of fairness should lead the police to conclude in favour of taping. It is, of course, also open to the police to tape-record interviews of persons outwith the scheme if they wish, although this should not use up machine time at the expense of other more serious cases. In the writer's experience, the police will sometimes tape-record a witness in a major enquiry if they anticipate the possibility of the witness being reluctant at a later stage and this seems good practice.

**6.30** The Thomson Committee's extreme stance that an unrecorded interview should be inadmissible has not been adopted. Where tape-recording is not practicable, for example because no tape-recorder is available or there has been a mechanical failure, statements should be noted in notebooks in the usual way, along with an explanation of the circumstances, since the officer may be required to justify in court his decision not to tape-record. If initially no recording can be made but one later becomes possible, there is no reason why comments or answers previously made cannot be put to the suspect on tape and the police are advised that such a practice might be 'helpful and/or desirable'.

**6.31** Fears about tampering are overcome by the provision of sophisticated twin-deck cassette recorders with each of the two tapes carrying two tracks, one of which records the interview and the other the time signal.

**6.32** Tape-recording is to be done overtly. Before commencing the interview the seals on the tapes are to be broken in the presence of the suspect and one tape placed in each machine. Thereafter the interviewing officer is to state the time and date, identify himself (including rank and force), state the location where the interview is taking place and name any other persons in the room. The suspect will then be asked to identify himself and once he has done so he will be cautioned. The suspect should be allowed to make as full a reply to the caution as he wishes. If he indicates that, rather than answering questions, he wishes to give an account in his own words he should be allowed to do so.

**6.33**  If a suspect refuses to be recorded the refusal should, if possible, be tape-recorded. If this is not possible, the police officers should note the refusal in their notebooks and the suspect should be invited to sign the notebooks to confirm his unwillingness to be tape-recorded. If the suspect indicates that he is willing to answer questions, but not while being recorded, the interviewing officer should point out to him that the recording is designed to protect the interests of the suspect and that any answers given remain subject to caution. However, if the suspect persists in his refusal, the tape-recorded interview should be concluded.

**6.34**  Similarly, if a suspect in the course of an interview states that he is not prepared to continue answering questions on tape, the police should try to persuade him to allow the tape-recorder to remain switched on. He should be told that he will have an opportunity to give any information he wishes unrecorded after the tape has been switched off at the end of the interview. However, if the suspect is adamant, the taped interview should be concluded immediately.

**6.35**  The caution and charge and any resulting reply should be tape-recorded and thereafter no further questions should be put to the suspect. If he wishes to make a voluntary statement, he should be afforded the opportunity to do so on tape. If he prefers to write it out, the tape should be left running while he writes it, and thereafter he can either have it read over to him or read it out himself. The normal rules for the taking of a voluntary statement[1] are to be followed even though the proceedings are being tape-recorded.

1 Para 6.04 above.

**6.36**  If it is decided to interrupt the interview, it should be concluded and the tape sealed, unless it is anticipated that the break will be short, for example a visit to the lavatory. In the latter case the tape will normally be stopped (with an appropriate explanation) and restarted after the interruption, although the tape may also be left running and an explanation given for the break in the interview.

**6.37**  Before the recorder is switched off, the interviewing officer should again state the time, day and date, details of those individuals present in the room and the location of the interview. Thereafter both tapes should be removed from the machine and placed in their cases. One of the tapes is to be sealed in the sight of the suspect, with a label signed by him and both the interviewing officers, and forwarded to the procurator fiscal as soon as possible. The other tape remains with the police. Only the fiscal or a designated member of his staff is permitted to break the seal. If no report is made to the fiscal, the sealed tape is to be kept by the police in a lockfast place separate from the police copy.

**6.38** Where judicial examination is anticipated, the police should make a note of the relevant questions and answers, and this should accompany the report to the procurator fiscal. The suspect's answers must be reported verbatim although the questions may be paraphrased.

**6.39** If the recording equipment malfunctions, the interviewing officer should try to record on tape the reasons why the interview is being terminated and bring it to an end, as nearly as possible in accordance with the normal practice. If another machine is available the interview may resume using a new tape. Where there is no alternative, the officer may resume the interview off tape, but he should be prepared to justify his decision in court.

**6.40** At the end of the interview the police should ensure that the police copy of the tape has voice-recording, and if it is found to be blank, that should be reported to the fiscal. The interviewing officers will then have to provide such account of the interview as they can from notes and memory.

**6.41** Defence solicitors were initally only permitted to listen to the tape in the office of the procurator fiscal and were not allowed to receive a copy of the tape either on loan or for retention. However, this has now been relaxed and procurators fiscal will supply copies of interview tapes to the defence on request.

**6.42** Unlike the position in England, the police in Scotland have no responsibility for the transcription of interview tapes, which lies with the procurator fiscal. There is no legal requirement for the fiscal to transcribe the tape and the court cannot insist on a transcript being available.[1] If the fiscal decides to transcribe the tape and to use the transcript in evidence, a copy may be served on the accused not less than 14 days before the trial and if the accused does not challenge its accuracy, it becomes admissible and sufficient evidence of the making of the transcript and its accuracy and does not require to be spoken to by witnesses.[2] If the accused does challenge the accuracy of the transcript, and the transcriber has to be called to give evidence, his uncorroborated evidence is sufficient of the making of the transcript and its accuracy.[3]

1 *McGlennan v McLaughlin* 1992 SCCR 454.
2 Criminal Justice (Scotland) Act 1987, s 60(1) and (2).
3 Ibid, s 60(4).

**6.43** No clear guidance has yet been given by the High Court as to the procedure to be followed when a tape and/or a transcript contains material which is prejudicial or inadmissible, such as a reference to previous convictions or to matters not charged on the indictment. The only case dealing with this point is *Tunnicliffe v HM Advocate*[1] which is unclear and unhelpful. In practice the prosecution and defence will normally agree an edited version of the transcript which will then be laid before the court by joint minute under section 150 or 354 of the Criminal Procedure (Scotland) Act 1975. If it is essential for the tape to be played, provided the parties agree, it will be played up to the point of the inadmissible material, run past it and then restarted. If the parties encounter difficulty in reaching agreement on an appropriate way of dealing with the inadmissible material it would be open to either side to seek a preliminary diet under section 76(1)(c) of the 1975 Act.[2]

1 1991 SCCR 623; para 6.46 below.
2 Cf *Styr v HM Advocate* 1993 SCCR 278.

**6.44** Since tape-recording is a comparatively recent innovation, there have been few cases so far where it has been an issue in its own right. The earliest case was *Swift v HM Advocate*[1] a rambling and somewhat unworldly sheriff court judgment arising from the Falkirk experiment. Most of the points which the sheriff considered possible problems have been dealt with by legislation and *Swift* is of little practical value nowadays. However, *Swift* did establish the slightly self-evident point that oral evidence of what was said and the tape-recording thereof were equally evidence of the same fact and hence two ways of proving the same thing.

1 1983 SCCR 204.

**6.45** Reference has previously been made to *Lord Advocate's Reference (No 1 of 1983)*[1] which is primarily an authority on the general issue of fairness rather than the specific question of tape-recording. However, the *Reference* did establish the important principle that:

'the presence in a transcript of an interview with a suspect under caution of certain answers which, for a sound reason, must be withheld from a jury will not by itself normally justify a trial judge in excluding from the jury's consideration the remainder of the transcript.'

1 1984 SCCR 62.

**6.46** *Tunnicliffe v HM Advocate*[1] is something of a curiosity. The circumstances were that the accused had been apprehended in Colchester and interviewed on tape there. In addition to clear admissions of the crimes with which he was indicted, the taped interview contained references to crimes in England which were, of course, not before the Scottish jury. The prosecution sought to make use of what would appear to have been an English transcript which had been edited so as to contain only references to the charges on the indictment. The defence apparently sought to allege that the entire Colchester interview had been unfair and as a preliminary to this objected to the edited transcript, which objection the sheriff upheld. Thereafter, the procurator fiscal sought to play the whole of the tape and despite defence objections the sheriff allowed this to be done leaving the question of prejudice to be dealt with in his charge to the jury. Having been convicted, the accused appealed.

1 1991 SCCR 623.

**6.47** At the appeal, the Crown indicated that it was not proposing to support the conviction and the appeal was accordingly allowed. The fact that the interview had been conducted in England in accordance with English practice was clearly a major complication, and one of the main reasons for the Crown's position, but the High Court made certain further observations of more general application which are, with respect, rather less than helpful. Although their Lordships accepted that 'in principle there is nothing objectionable to editing a transcript if it is capable of being so edited', they went on to say:

'It is not impossible, we should have thought, for a tape to be edited in such a way that all those passages which could result in prejudice to the accused are excluded when the tape is played in precisely the same way as passages are excluded from the verbatim written record which is lodged as a production. . . . So if the Crown is intending to lodge . . . the tape recording of an interview which contains material which may have to be excluded on the ground of unfairness it should provide the machinery and make all the necessary preparations so that an edited version of the recording can be played.'

**6.48** Taken literally, the implications of this statement are worrying. It is to be hoped that all that their Lordships were suggesting was that arrangements should be made along the lines previously discussed[1] but that is not what was actually said. It is submitted that it would be contrary to interests of justice for the courts to encourage any form of tampering with the actual interview tape. It is one thing to edit a transcript while preserving the tape intact but it is entirely another matter to suggest that (presumably) the prosecution should physically alter an important piece of evidence. It is something of a relief to note an *obiter dictum* in *Carmichael v Boyd*[2] which refers to *Tunnicliffe* as having decided that 'The transcript of an interview may be edited so as to withhold from a jury passages in it which are inadmissible'. This is clearly a welcome interpretation but it is not an accurate reflection of what was said in *Tunnicliffe* and it is unlikely to be the final word on this important issue.

1 Para 6.43 above.
2 1993 SCCR 751 at 758C.

**6.49**  The only other decision concerning tape-recording to date is *Hudson v Hamilton*[1] in which it was held that in the absence of any dispute as to the contents of the tape, the fairness of the interview, or any other problems, there was no need for the tape to be played while the second interviewing police officer was giving his evidence, the tape having already been played during the evidence of the first interviewing officer. It was sufficient for the second officer to identify the tape as the one used to record what was said during the interview.

1 1992 SCCR 541.

### Video-recording

**6.50**  Although tape-recording is undoubtedly a great step forwards in providing for an accurate record, it is sometimes suggested that video-recording would be even better since it enables the demeanour of the suspect to be observed and it can assist even more than the tape in protecting the police from false allegations of violence or threats thereof.

**6.51**  The courts already have experience of the use of video-recordings from various sources. Video-tapes from security cameras and the like are routinely played in Scottish courts, the paucity of reported cases suggesting that few problems are encountered, and recordings made by television companies have been admitted in Scotland.[1] The police themselves already make use of video-cameras for matters such as surveillance and recording the locus of a crime, and police traffic patrol cars are sometimes fitted with video-cameras for the purpose of recording aberrant driving. It is also common for officers carrying out drugs raids to video their actions in order to forestall challenges and allegations of 'planting'. As a matter of technology there would seem to be no reason why a scheme for video-recording of police interviews could not be introduced virtually at once. The only legislative provision necessary would appear to be the widening of section 60 of the Criminal Justice (Scotland) Act 1987[2] to allow for the transcription of the soundtrack of a video-recording.

1 *Macphail* § 13.12. For a practical description of the use of video-recordings in an English case see M S Barnes 'One Experience of Video Recorded Interviews' [1993] Crim LR 444.
2 Para 6.42 above.

**6.52** There have been experiments with video-recordings in other jurisdictions, the results of which have generally been encouraging. A Canadian experiment has shown that, like tape-recording, video-recording does not appear to inhibit suspects from making confessions and admissions, and very few suspects decline to be interviewed on tape. It also showed, if that were necessary, that there was no evidence that costly professional camera crews or other technical assistance was necessary to produce a clear and reliable record of the interview.[1] An English experiment has also yielded generally positive results although there is also a certain amount of evidence of a disturbing tendency on the part of some officers to indulge in 'informal' off-camera interrogation of the suspect leading to the video-recording giving a totally false impression of what had taken place.[2]

1 A Grant 'Videotaping Police Questioning: A Canadian Experiment' [1987] Crim LR 375.
2 M McConville 'Videotaping Interrogations' [1992] Crim LR 532; see also H Fenwick 'Confessions, Recording Rules and Miscarriages of Justice' [1993] Crim LR 174.

**6.53** Apart from interviews in the police station, the writer would also suggest that the police could, with advantage, consider video-recording the actions of an accused person who voluntarily takes them out of the police station for the purpose of showing them houses into which he has broken, where he had discarded a weapon, or the like. Such evidence is frequently attacked on the basis that the police knew all along the address of the premises or the place of concealment and the locus visit was merely a charade. A video-recording would go a long way towards proving where the truth lies.

## SOME OBSERVATIONS

**6.54** No method of recording a confession is wholly proof against possible police malpractice. Tape- and video-recording represent a

considerable improvement on written notes and it is admittedly difficult to figure a situation where a tape- or video-recording could be an
outright fabrication. The real danger lies in what happens outwith the
reach of the microphone or camera, as became apparent from the early
research into the Scottish tape-recording experiment.[1] Recent
English experience has shown that if it is possible for them to do so the
police are liable to indulge in informal 'softening up' of the suspect
before putting him on tape or camera. An apparently relaxed and
spontaneous interview might well be the result of flagrant abuse of a
system designed to protect the suspect's rights.[2] Although there are
many differences in police practices in Scotland, it would at the very
least be naive to discount the possibility of similar behaviour by Scottish officers.

1 Para 6.23 above.
2 M McConville 'Videotaping Interrogations' [1992] Crim LR 532; Royal Commission
  on Criminal Justice Research Study No 22 (HMSO, 1993).

**6.55**  A recent English study of some 600 tape transcripts yielded
some fascinating results and in particular showed that the standard of
police interviewing was poor, leading the author to observe that 'the
image of police interviewers as professional, skilled and forceful inter-
rogators scarcely matched the reality'.[1] A properly conducted programme of research into the interviewing practices of Scottish police
officers is long overdue and in the absence of such research it is impossible to know how good or otherwise Scottish police officers are at
interviewing suspects. However, even a limited study of a random
selection of Scottish interview transcripts would tend to suggest that
several of Professor Baldwin's findings are applicable in Scotland.
Nevertheless, generalisation from the particular and extrapolation
from English findings are liable to lead to conclusions which are
unjustifiable in the Scottish situation and it is to be hoped that the
means will be found to mount a proper study of this vital area of the
criminal process.

1 J Baldwin 'Police Interview Techniques' (1993) 33 Br J Crim 325.

# Index

# Index

# Index

Legal persons, admissions by, 3.09
Letter, confession in, admissibility of, 2.164, 2.165

Magistrate, right to interrogate, historically, 1.07
Medical adviser, confession to, 2.150–2.152
Mental capacity, effect on admissibility, 2.114–2.116, 2.163
Minister, confession to, 2.155–2.161, 5.13
Mixed statements
  current position, 3.23–3.34
  generally, 1.23, 3.10
  historical background, 3.11–3.22

Non-verbal confessions, 1.24–1.26, 2.45, 3.06, 3.38

Objection, requirement for timeous, 2.167
Overheard statements, admissibility of, 2.117–2.125, 2.129, 6.18

Police
  caution. *See* CAUTION
  confessions,
    historical background,
      1800s, 2.23–2.32
      1900–1920s, 2.33–2.35
      1920s–1950s, 2.35–2.39
      1950s, 2.40–2.53
      1960s, 2.54–2.63
      1970s, 2.64–2.75
      1980s, 2.76, 2.77
  deception, 2.30, 2.118, 2.122–2.125, 2.148, 3.05
  detention. *See* DETENTION
  eavesdropping by, 2.117–2.125, 6.18
  improper conduct, effect of, 1.29, 2.30, 2.118–2.125, 2.148, 3.05
  informers, use of, 2.122, 2.148
  judicial scepticism of, origins, 2.24, 2.26 ff
  notebooks, 6.03, 6.09–6.13
  recording equipment, use of. *See* TAPE-RECORDING, VIDEO-RECORDING
  right to silence at interview, 1.18, 1.19
  'verballing'. *See* FABRICATED CONFESSIONS

Police – *contd*
  voluntary statements, 1.07, 1.27, 2.78, 2.92
    *See also* EXTRA-JUDICIAL CONFESSIONS, FAIRNESS TEST
Police surgeon, confession to, 2.150, 2.151
Preliminary diet, consideration of admissibility at, 4.19, 6.43
Priest, confession to, 2.155–2.161, 5.13
Prison officer, confession to, 2.127, 2.128
Prisoner
  confession to, 2.129
  letter by, admissibility of, 2.164, 2.165
  sleeping, confession by, 2.163
Private persons, confessions to, 2.135, 2.143–2.149
Procedure
  solemn. *See* SOLEMN PROCEDURE
  summary. *See* SUMMARY PROCEDURE
  trial within a trial. *See* TRIAL WITHIN A TRIAL
  voluntary statements, 2.92, 6.20
Procurator fiscal, Scottish tape-recording scheme, and, 6.37, 6.38, 6.40, 6.41, 6.42
Prosecution. *See* CROWN
Public officials and investigators, confessions to, 2.130–2.142

Qualified confessions. *See* MIXED STATEMENTS

Recent possession of stolen property, 1.21
Record of confession. *See* EXTRA-JUDICIAL CONFESSION
Relevancy, generally, 1.28, 1.29
Religious adviser, confession to, 2.155–2.162, 5.13
Right to silence
  adverse judicial comments, 1.16, 1.17, 3.25
  adverse prosecution comments, 1.15, 1.17
  England and Wales, 1.12
  historical background, 1.13–1.17
  judicial examination and, 1.17
  meaning, 1.11
  police interview, at, 1.18, 1.19
  self-incrimination privilege contrasted, 1.11

# Index